THE JOYFUL JOURNEY

WOMEN OF FAITH℠

THE JOYFUL JOURNEY

PATSY CLAIRMONT BARBARA JOHNSON

MARILYN MEBERG LUCI SWINDOLL

with JANET KOBOBEL GRANT

ZondervanPublishingHouse

Grand Rapids, Michigan

A Division of HarperCollinsPublishers

The Joyful Journey
Copyright © 1997 by Patsy Clairmont, Barbara Johnson, Marilyn Meberg, and
Luci Swindoll

Requests for information should be addressed to:

📖 ZondervanPublishingHouse
Grand Rapids, Michigan 49530

Library of Congress Cataloging-in-Publication Data

The joyful journey / Patsy Clairmont ... [et al.].
     p.   cm.
    ISBN 0-310-21344-4
     1. Christian women—Religious life.   2. Women—Conduct of life.
  I. Clairmont, Patsy.
  BV4527.J68   1997
  248.8'43—dc21   96-39584
                                                  CIP

Scripture quotations are from:

The Holy Bible, New International Version (NIV), © 1973, 1984 by the
International Bible Society. Used by permission of Zondervan Publishing House;

New American Standard Bible (NASB), © 1960, 1977 by the Lockman Foundation;

The New King James Version (NKJV), © 1984 by Thomas Nelson, Inc.;

The King James Version (KJV);

The Living Bible (TLB), © 1971 by Tyndale House Publishers;

The Message, © 1993 by Eugene H. Peterson;

The Revised Standard Version Bible (RSV), © 1946, 1952, 1971 by the Division of
Christian Education of the National Council of Churches of Christ in the USA.
Used by permission.

If We Could See Beyond Today © 1943 by Norman Clayton Publishing Co. (a
division of Word, Inc.) All rights reserved. Used by permission.

This edition is printed on acid-free paper and meets the American National
Standards Institute Z39.48 standard.

Interior design by Sherri L. Hoffman

Printed in the United States of America

---

98 99 00 01 02 03 04 /❖ DC/ 17 16 15 14 13 12 11

Contents

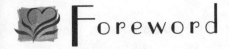

Foreword

Have you ever given a gift that was so right, so from the heart, and so surprising that you couldn't wait to deliver it? To see it opened, to see the eyes of the receiver light up with delight, is a gift to the giver. The Women of Faith organization feels that way about you and this book. We know the surprise that the Women of Faith conferences has been for thousands of women all across the country. The speakers have delighted and encouraged the hearts of women from all walks of life and from all denominations. We know about the joy each attendee expresses as she is revisited by God in meaningful and powerful ways while she listens to Patsy, Barbara, Marilyn, and Luci. We know that, as you travel through these pages with these very special women, the same experiences await you. Be prepared as you read to be entertained, to be encouraged, to be inspired, to be surprised, and most of all to be reminded that God is at work around you and in you pointing out the way with "road signs."

Jeremiah 31:21b says, "Set up road signs; put up guideposts. Take note of the highway, the road that you take" (NKJV). It is our desire at Women of Faith to see women live as fully as God intends for each of them. We want to bring light to the path and to be a source of encouragement and inspiration, always pointing the way back to God and the importance of our relationship with him. This book is one manifestation of that desire. As you read, ask God to open your eyes to the signs he is using in your life, whether he is asking you today to Slow Down or to Watch for Falling Rocks, or if, for this season, he is gently pulling you into the tutelage of the School Zone.

In the past year, as we have journeyed with these four women, we have found them to be unendingly fun, deeply caring, and invaluable traveling companions. They are the most authentic women we know. The kinship they feel for each other is obvious on every page of this book, just as it is at each conference. They are true Women of Faith, and if you don't know them now, you will take each one of them to your heart as you walk these roads with them.

We invite you now to join hands with us as we "take note of the highway" together.

Pamela McCann
Women of Faith

Setting Out

by Patsy, Barbara, Marilyn, and Luci

A joyful journey. A tantalizing trip. A wondrous wandering. That's what life is all about. Not that only blissful events unfold for us. Not that all splendid sunrises and sunsets capsulize life. Quite the contrary. Dips, bends, swerves, and curves typify life. But what happens to our interior as our exterior wends its way through the time and space God has given us to experience? Do we become hardened, bitter, and downright harmful to ourselves and others? Or do we let God bend low over us to console us and to bring us joy as we travel through life?

Certainly, we have examples of both in Scripture. But have you ever noticed how many soul-defining moments occurred to biblical characters—and we do mean *characters*—as they traveled? Jacob rushed away from betraying his brother, camped out on the road, and dreamed of a ladder that led to heaven. When it was time for him to pack up from his years of self-inflicted exile, he encountered an angel on the return trip. As they wrestled, Jacob was touched in a deep—and wounding—way. He lurched toward home with the mark of God on him.

Adam and Eve were sent on an arduous journey from which they could never return after their misadventures in the Garden. Abraham and Lot embarked on a major relocation, and the choices they made brought one of them closer to the bosom of God and took the other away, causing him to be spiritually lost. David lived the life of a nomad while the king hunted him—and David's heart was strengthened in his homeless years.

What could be more momentous or frightening than to give birth while you're traveling? Yet, that's just what happened to Mary and Joseph. They, too, found themselves in exile, fleeing to Egypt to save their precious son—and God's. All of this while they were adrift from their moorings, far from family, from home, from comfort and stability. But close, ever so close, to God himself.

Jesus was a wanderer, but even he took a special journey to commence his ministry and spent forty days in the wilderness. After his death, it was on a road, the one to Emmaus, where he appeared to two of his disciples.

The road is, therefore, in many ways a fitting symbol for the pinnacles and pits we encounter in life. As with the men and women we meet in the Bible, we, too, can reach home with our souls strengthened from our travels. Full of joy because we have seen God afresh. Able to identify with Job, who once saw "the fringes" of God's ways, but after a painful inner journey, "saw" God as he never had before. Scripture heartens us and assures us our travels are not without purpose. Many have traveled this path before us. We can learn from them the way to go so that we, too, will complete the trip spiritually stronger than when we first met Jesus on the road. (Rather like Paul, who had an eye-opening conversion on the road.)

With this heritage of wanderings, we four travelers set out on a journey of our own: to write about the joys, despairs, happiness, and sorrows all of us encounter along the way. As modern travelers, it occurred to us that we have received guidance on our trip through road signs. They tell us what's up ahead and how to prepare for it. They have warned us to expect Soft Shoulders, Falling Rocks, No Outlet, School Crossing, and Curves Ahead. As well, we have encountered a few unexpected postings such as Drive Friendly, Duck Crossing, and Men at Work. What do they all mean? That's what we plan to tell you. And we hope you'll find a giggle or two along the way, as well as an insight or two. Climb in, buckle up, and prepare for the trip of your life—because that's really what life is.

One

Soft Shoulder

Patsy Clairmont

Traveling in the company of those we love is home in motion.
—LEIGH HUNT

I've been laughing myself, not silly, but sane on the Joyful Journey. My cohorts in chortling, Barbara, Marilyn, and Luci, have reminded me to look for the joy along this journey called life. And don't we find joy in some of the most startling places: in embarrassing moments, in mistakes, in the hands of an enemy, between the Tidy Bowl and the toothpaste in the grocery aisle, at the doctor's office, in the throes of debt, on a soft shoulder during painful times. Who'd a thunk it? Joy in spite of life—what potential that holds for this labyrinth we are in, this winding road that ultimately leads us home. But until we arrive on heaven's sod (Is there sod in heaven? How about celestial turf?), we sure could use some highway signs to keep us on the right road. I'd like mine billboard size. Preferably neon. Large-print edition.

My husband, Les (alias Hopalong Clairmont), knows the danger that exists without the benefit of a well-placed sign. For several years he worked at a youth facility as director of maintenance. On one camp project, Les and some others built a road across a swamp so as to more easily access picnic areas on the grounds. (Similar to the way a mom bulldozes a path from the kids' rooms to the dinner table.)

One day Hopalong was driving a sixty-passenger, flat-nosed bus down the new road when suddenly the shoulder gave way and the bus lurched left. The driver's side of the vehicle tipped forward and then downward, and the bus began to sink. Les, feeling highly motivated to evacuate the premises, galloped to the back exit and leapt out. He obviously was more of a cowboy than a captain because he was not about to go down with the ship.

On a nearby hillside a group of youth waiting to ride a zip line spotted Les's crisis, formed a posse, and hightailed it to his rescue. When the wrecking service arrived some time later, the men found sixteen laughing teenage boys dangling from the bus windows using their weight to counterbalance the water's pull on the tottering yellow beast. This team effort prevented the bus from drowning in the swamp and becoming a Jacques Cousteau artifact. Four tentative hours later the baptized bus made it onto solid ground.

Les definitely needed a Soft Shoulder road sign. Such warnings alert us to a fragile roadside—one that can support weight but, when overtaxed, begins to crumble.

Do I ever identify! I, too, have crumbly edges when I try to support ... say ... the weight of the world (or a busload of needy people). This tendency may be innately packaged inside most women. We long to connect with others and to nurture them, sometimes allowing too many to park on our soft shoulders.

Yet I prize those qualities within us—our interest in relationships at deep levels and our ability to nudge, encourage, and promote well-being. In fact, I just love being a woman. I like to fuss with lace, ruffles, teacups, and roses. I am pleased with an attractive outfit, a soft hairstyle, a sweet fragrance, and a genteel manner. I take delight in shopping, gardening, decorating, and luncheon rendezvous. At the same time, I get a kick out of biking, baseball games, pinball machines, and roller blading as playful diversions. Music also is a moving part of my womanly world—from Beethoven to Broadway to Beebop. I can move quickly from a psalm to a sonata to Sinatra to Sam Cook in a flick of my CD changer. I also can go from smiling to sniveling to sizzling in a flash.

I am complex; at times I am a contradiction, occasionally I am a cacophony of emotions, and more frequently I am content and, yes, even confident as a tender counterpart.

These feminine nuances make us mysterious (even to ourselves) as well as mainstays to those traveling along life's highway looking for a place to pull off. A woman's soft shoulder suggests rest, comfort, shelter, and relief. A woman's shoulder can absorb teardrops, quake with mutual laughter, be a harbor for secrets, and become a dispeller of fears. Add to that the workloads women shoulder, many alone, and we catch a glimpse of the versatility, virtues, and verve of womanhood. I love being a woman!

That is not to say that being a woman doesn't have its corresponding inconveniences. Mascara applicators, high heels, and clip earrings all have a way of leaving indelible imprints on the female species. Not to mention the difficulties of nail polish, pantyhose, and permanents. (One permanent left me looking like Orphan Annie's less fortunate sister.) The smell of the beauty salon solutions alone is enough to addle the brain. Then there is the curling iron, a quick answer to instant tattooing. More than once I have resembled a stray calf with a brand clearly smoldered into my neck. I know a woman who developed a hernia from lifting her cosmetic case. I personally have been forced to trade in my zippered cosmetic pouch for a duffel bag. My neighbor changed her hair color four times in the last two weeks in an effort to find the one that would please her husband. They finally settled on a burgundy with purplish highlights. What we women go through for ourselves, for other women, and for the men in this world. No wonder some of us grow strong in the process.

And some of the strongest women I know have the softest shoulders. My four-foot-ten-inch momma is a formidable gal. There is not much she can't do. Her mindset? The higher the mountain, the more exhilarating the climb. Over the years I've watched her attack tough jobs with spit and vigor and deal with difficult people with strength and spunkiness. Mom's slight stature has never impeded her ability to hold her own in the face of even the tallest of challenges. Whether it's entertaining strangers (one time, unassisted, she prepared five-course dinners in our home every night for a week for twelve missionaries), ministering to the grieving (after living in the area two weeks my mom opened our home to a neighboring family so they would have a place in which to meet and eat following the death of a loved one), or preparing for hours each week to teach a classroom of children about Jesus, my mom knows how to distribute her life-strength with purpose and grace. What stands out clearly in my mind are all the people who have sought out my mom's strong yet soft shoulder . . . including me.

Now, when I say the word *strong* I don't mean "obnoxious," and when I say *soft*, I'm certainly not suggesting weak. I am unimpressed with bossy broads and wimpy whiners. I find those attributes unattractive and unappealing—even though . . . ahem . . . I have been both in given situations. No, I am referring to women who are confident but not caustic, definite yet teachable, intelligent but not haughty, supportive without being indulgent, humorous yet not foolish, disciplined but not controlling, and merciful without being sappy.

I realize this sounds like quite the tall order. Of course, none of us can be a perfect ten, but if you're like me, we could make a lot of improvements and still not be mistaken for the Proverbs 31 woman.

It seems that our tendency, if we are strong, is to err toward abrasiveness, which diminishes our strength and hardens the shoulder we have to offer a hurting world. Who wants to rest her head against a brick wall? Ouch!

When I'm bewildered and overwhelmed, I seek the gentle guidance of a person I know will respond with compassion. Life is complicated enough without having to listen to the caustic remarks of someone's misdirected strength.

At times I have appropriately and even admirably offered my shoulder only to become so full of myself for my positive response that I short-circuited any personal growth I might have received from the experience. For instance, have you ever gone the extra sacrificial mile for someone close to you and then not mentioned it, not even to the person? You may have basked in the glow of your inner strength and maturity in the situation. Then, a month or a year later, in the midst of a heated discussion, you toss your unapplauded sacrifice in that person's face. Don't you hate it when that happens? I've done that. I've started off right and then pro-ceeded to smudge it up with my need for credit.

I have leaned on more than a few shoulders (even worn some out), both male and female, in my life's journey. I have leaned on more women's shoulders than men's, although, I must say, my hus-band's shoulder is usually the first one I seek out for comfort and counsel (even though I don't always agree with his offerings). From there I turn to a select circle of female friends for tender insights, gentle reproofs, and strong challenges (even though I don't always agree with their offerings). Hmm, there seems to be a recurring theme here.

I would love to tell you that I first run to the Lord for a shoul-der to cry on, to bolster my courage, and to find a balm for my bruised soul. But sometimes I am negligent, until all my other options are depleted. Then I remember. Gratefully, I know it is his plan that we extend ourselves to one another. Certainly not in place of him, but as a way to be honorably connected to each other through him.

I can imagine Elizabeth, soon-to-be mom of John the Baptist, drawing Mary, soon-to-be mother of Jesus, onto her aging shoulder. Two women, the old and the young, embracing in mutual identification. Two women seeking solace in each other's company. Two women honorably connecting to one another. Sisters of divine circumstance shouldering the future of humanity.

Those ladies changed history, but it's all I can do to keep my garden weeded, my closets tidy, and a lid on my verbiage. Life often overtakes me. I remember boohooing on my friend Ruthann's shoulder about my complicated lifestyle. It seemed my calendar was careening out of control, turning my joyful journey into a jarring one.

Ruthann, a wordsmith with a masterful vocabulary and exacting enunciation, decided I needed to expand my vocabulary. So she taught me the word *no*—a one-syllable, two-letter powerhouse that prevents us from being victimized by life's pressures and turmoils. I'd heard the word previously, but I just wasn't proficient in its use. Since incorporating this word, I've lost a few acquaintances and gained some (don't want to exaggerate) sanity. Nothing can compare to the feeling that we actually have some control over the direction our lives take; it's like mapping out our own journey.

(Time out: About maps. I'm so proud I have finally learned how to read them. I still get lost, but now I know where I am in my lostness . . . sorta. I do think maps would be more fun if each state were in a designer color and the malls were highlighted with iridescent orange dots. That way even at night one could still find one's way to the nearest Nordstrom. Also, as we traveled, we could enjoy connect-a-store from state to state. Then I think we should change the north, south, east, west arrows on maps to read Nieman Marcus, Spiegels, Eddie Bauer, Williams Sonoma. For we gals know that all roads eventually lead to the mall.)

Now, back to "no." At times I weaken, fall back into the fast track, and have to be tutored again in no's merits. It's almost as if I'm addicted to a pogo-stick existence.

I thank the Lord for Ruthann's soft shoulder and tough message. Let me repeat it for you; the word is "no." "No!" Got it? Okay, now you try it . . . go ahead. It gets easier with practice.

Practice is also important in reading road signs because one never knows what the next bend may bring. Why, we might run smack dab into a fuming neighbor, a boomerang child, or a tyrannical boss. It's at those times, especially when the neighbor, child, and boss all collide with us on the same day, that we need a sign directing us to a soft shoulder—the soft shoulder of a compatriot. Of course, it sometimes happens that the collision is with our compatriot. Yikes! This is particularly disconcerting. Quick, someone install a Stop sign! What do we do when the soft shoulder we can usually rely on turns cold?

First off, it's important to have more than one friend. Limiting ourselves to one "best friend" sets us up for emotional trauma when the friend leaves (through death, a move, etc.) or is no longer friendly (doesn't that hurt?). Besides, so many wacky, wonderful people are out there, just waiting to welcome us into their lives. Why not splurge and have a plethora of friends?

Jesus chose twelve disciples, but he seemed especially close to three of them—Peter, James, and John—and even closer yet to just one—John, whom he called Beloved. Perhaps this would be a good guideline for our friendships.

I've learned I can't be best buddies with as many as I'd like because time and life just don't permit it. But twelve dear friends, three of them close, and one of them especially dear . . . I can do that.

I must remember, though, that my circle of friends are human and will not always be there when I need them. In the Garden of Gethsemane, when Jesus sought out a soft shoulder, he found his disciples in la-la land. Z-z-z. They were too weary to care for anyone but themselves (been there, done that). In our humanness, we sometimes fail one another. This does not negate our need for friendship, but it does remind us to have realistic expectations of people's abilities and availabilities. It also reminds us that there is One who will rush to meet us like the prodigal's parent when he returned home. How can we feel forlorn with the assurance of that kind of joyful reception and warm embrace?

Even so, the Lord created us with an emotional and relational need for human contact. Nothing can hearten like the hug from a caring person.

My friend Shirley Valade is a joyous hugging machine. She brings cheer to others by her very entry into a room. Shirley, by example, taught me years ago to receive fully and to give freely a hug, a pat, and a soft shoulder.

I remember the time Shirley was assigned to be my hostess at a women's retreat. Now, the "normal" role of a hostess is to give the speaker a basket of fruit, a program, and if needed, a ride. Shirley went way beyond that. She brought me my own delicatessen in a picnic basket, including long tablecloth, candles, and lovely music. And if that were not enough, she brought a folding massage table and gave me back rubs between my sessions. I so appreciated her creative gestures, for I am a woman who enjoys being fussed over. Shirley is a woman of flair . . . and prayer. The sweetest gifts she gave me that weekend were the times she drew me to her shoulder and prayed God's blessing on me.

God *has* blessed me; and one of his blessings is my women friends. Women like Shirley, Ruthann, and the Joyful Journey trio—Barbara, Marilyn, and Luci. These "girls" from the Journey charge my batteries—they are imaginative, colorful, entertaining, and slightly off-center. Being rather off-tilt myself, the four of us make a good match.

We had never worked together as a team until the tour. At the first Joyful Journey event we were amazed at the solid connection we felt with one another. We quickly discovered that we not only work well together, but we also play well together. We have mutual respect for each other's gifts, we are quick to applaud each other's successes, and we laugh a lot.

One day, as Barbara and I chatted on the phone about a ridiculous yet innocent mistake I had made in one of my answers in a recent magazine interview, we started laughing. The longer we discussed my faux pas the harder we laughed until we were convulsing in giggles. Our guffawing immediately lightened my load and restored my joy. After that laugh-a-thon, I found I was freed from the stigma of my own ignorance and could move past my mistake.

More recently I became so tickled at one of Luci's stories, I was certain we would have to send out for a respirator and a case of Depends. Shrieking hysterically, I clung to a wall in our hotel as Luci attempted to retell an experience that had happened to our mutual friend Pat. Tears streamed down both our faces as we entered Pat's experience via Luci's gifted storytelling and the bridge of laughter. (I'm laughing even as I type this.) Afterward, I thought, *I love Luci.* Something about sharing a hooting laugh with another creates joy in friendship.

I have noticed an increased effort to actively look for the joy in my journey since globetrotting with these three deliriously delightful women. I'm learning to take myself less seriously and the Lord more seriously, which has compounded my joy. I have the capacity to be quite intense, inflating minuscule into monumental in a couple of hot breaths. The Joy team helps me reevaluate my responses by their responses.

For instance, a move from one geographical location to another is, for me, earthshaking, mind-boggling, emotionally disconcerting, and physically fraying. Well, recently Marilyn moved. Even though her move was by choice, it was still a huge upheaval in many ways; it meant a change in weather, work, and home size. I watched. I waited. I listened.

What a trooper Marilyn is. What an example. What a road sign! She faced the difficulty, disruption, and new location with a sense of adventure and humor. Not that it was pain free for her. Marilyn openly voiced her adjustment struggles but without whining. This was particularly impressive because I have trouble moving my couch from one side of the room to the other without whining. And we do learn from one another. Sooner than I would have liked, I will be able to apply myself what I learned from Marilyn. I just found out I'm going to . . . move.

We may not always realize how many around us are observing our responses. We are like walking, talking road signs. And when we are staked deep in the soil of faith, we can help point others toward joy. "This is the way; walk ye in it."

Remember, a woman naturally extends herself to others, which can bring joy or lead to edginess. When I take on too much, my soft shoulder begins to cave in. Yet when I'm emotionally unavailable, I lose the deep satisfaction that comes when I offer a soft and compassionate shoulder to others in their time of need. Knowing my limitations keeps me relating, while preventing me from crumbling under too much pressure. Most of all, it allows me the joy of being a woman.

Join us as we (Barbara, Marilyn, Luci, and I) share with you some of the other signs that lead to joy.

 Two

Curves Ahead

Marilyn Meberg

It's a long lane that knows no turnings.
—ROBERT BROWNING

I'm mystified by the deadly intensity of many golfers. The game of golf is meant to be relaxing, rejuvenating, and restorative. It's generally played on courses that have carefully manicured greens, multicolored flowers, and trees so inviting one would love to stop and picnic for an hour. Or, if pressed for time, just lie on one's back, luxuriating in the grass, gazing at the sky through tree branches. One could create creatures in cloud formations or simply breathe in the surrounding lushness. The golf course presents endless possibilities for the enrichment of one's soul.

The majority of golfers, however, don't share my view. Many of them see golf as the opportunity to show off their agility and competence, to prove their personal value and worth, perhaps even to demonstrate to others that "I am a person to be reckoned with. After all, I got on the green in just one shot."

I remember the time a number of years ago when my husband, Ken (who passed away in 1990), and I were teamed up with two of these deadly-intense-type of golfers. We had never met this couple before; we were simply assigned to them so we could go out on the course as a foursome. Only a few moments into the game I realized what we were in for. I immediately noticed the rule book on the dashboard of their golf cart, and I also presumed, by the cadaverous set to their faces, that smiling while playing was a definite no-no. I groaned inwardly, knowing they wouldn't take kindly to my habit of kicking the ball inbounds or taking any number of shots until the ball went where I wanted it to.

The game proceeded mirthlessly except for the stolen giggles Ken and I shared with each other. Actually, by the time we reached the seventh hole on the front nine, I was having a delightful time in spite of the funereal atmosphere in the cart that followed us. As it came time for me to tee off, I decided that the lure of the sand trap was sufficiently far away and I could dare to play my "pink lady." If not, I would have played a white ball; dull and expendable.

You see, one of my favorite aspects of golf is these gorgeous little pink balls called "Flying Ladies." When the pink ball is nestled in the green grass the contrast of colors pleases me enormously. Some golf balls are bright orange or chartreuse and totally offensive. For the sake of aesthetics, I think they should be banned from play. However, the little pink balls do have one distinct disadvantage. They are basically beach balls; they love sand and water.

I made the shot with my usually trustworthy three-iron and to my horror, the pink lady did a ninety-degree turn, sailing over my right shoulder and clattering noisily on the Spanish tiled roof of a fairway condominium. I heard the ball hit the cement patio, and then all was quiet.

The fun couple turned disdainfully away, pretending they had not witnessed such a spectacle. I would have felt so much better if they had laughed heartily and declared that to be the worst shot they had ever seen. This response was, of course, not in their repertoire.

Ken, in an effort to rescue me, came over and whispered, "Just hit another ball, Marilyn, and we'll play on."

"Babe, I can't hit another ball. That was a pink lady!"

Ken knew my inordinate attachment to these balls and simply nodded when I told him to go on, that I would catch up later after I had found "her." I searched all over the patio where I had seen her bounce, lifting patio chair cushions, parting the shrubbery with my three-iron and, even scanning the neighbor's patio. Not a sign of her. Then I noticed that the condo's slider door leading from the patio to the living room was open about a foot. I stared into the depths of that room and couldn't believe what I saw. There, tucked between the second and third cushions of an ugly brown couch, was my pink lady. I couldn't help but think, *What a shot. That really was far more extraordinary than a hole in one!*

"Hello," I called out hesitantly, then louder, "Hello!" Hearing no answer, I took off my golf shoes so I could stealthily make my way across the room to retrieve my ball and then slip away. (It would be tacky to wear spiked golf shoes in the home of a perfect stranger.) I was practically to the couch when an elderly gentleman emerged from the kitchen. He stopped abruptly, as did I.

"I'm so sorry," I said sheepishly. "Please forgive me for coming into your home this way, but you see the little pink golf ball on your couch? She's mine."

He looked mildly amused, then reached over to the cushion and scooped up my ball. "No, my dear," he said, "this is not your ball. This condo is mine, the couch is mine, and anything that sits on this couch is mine. So you see, that means this pretty little ball is mine." I felt a rush of protective emotion and intended to plead for the release of my pink lady when he laughed warmly, tossed her to me, and said, "You might have better luck playing tennis."

I decided against telling him about my equally extraordinary tennis shots. I thanked him and fled.

At times I feel as if the events of my life are riding on a pink golf ball that suddenly curves off in a direction I didn't plan, didn't want, and over which I have no control. In dismay, I watch as my life careens off the course I have carefully planned for it. And, as in my rescue of the pink golf ball, I have to wander off my chosen course to reinstitute my life. While this is an adventuresome experience, it is not a selected or joyous one.

I've also experienced many unexpected curves that *were* delightful and enriching. I didn't see them coming, nor did I have time to prepare; they were just suddenly there.

One such curve has been the onset of the Joyful Journey conferences. When the plan was first presented to me that I join Patsy, Barbara, and Luci in a series of conferences to be held in different cities all over the country, I thought, *What a dynamite idea and what an incomparable trio of women with whom to minister!*

My friendship with Luci has spanned more than twenty years, and I have known and loved Barbara for at least ten years. What a treat to be with them. I was, of course, familiar with Patsy's fine reputation as well as her equally fine books, but we had never met. I looked forward to that enormously. I anticipated a smooth working relationship would develop among all of us, but I admit I hadn't anticipated the depth of kinship we would so quickly develop. We openly and warmly respect each other as speakers, are quick to give affirmation and support and, amazingly, haven't tired of hearing each other in spite of the by-now-familiar material. We care for each other in not only what concerns the Joyful Journey conferences but also in what affects our personal lives. I talk to Luci, Barbara, and Patsy several times a week and sometimes several times a day.

Patsy and I share an enjoyable curve in that we have similar tastes in food—various pastas, garlic, chocolate, peach cobbler, etc. Because I'm not terribly disciplined about anything chocolate, I frequently order dessert if the chocolate whatever is too tempting to resist. Patsy, on the other hand, rarely orders dessert.

However, when my dessert is served, Patsy will wordlessly lift her fork into the ready position. Early on in our travels, I offered her a standing invitation to "take a bite" should she wish. Now we usually confer before we even order—on all menu items.

When we were in Denver once, I intended to order a pasta dish and she a vegetable plate. As I started to give my order, Patsy leaned over and whispered, "Be sure to tell them to go light on the garlic. We speak tonight." Of course I complied. When she gave her order, I whispered, "Tell them not to overcook the vegetables. I hate mushy vegetables." When the food arrived we divvied up our respective orders so that we each had a share of not-too-mushy vegetables and lightly garlicked pasta. Now don't you think there's something homey and warm about a couple of little old ladies gumming their food together in companionable collaboration? I love that curve.

Another part of the Joyful Journey experience that has thrown us all a wonderful curve is the enthusiastic response of the nation's women at our conferences. When Steve Arterburn of New Life Clinics conceived the idea to put four speakers on tour with the unifying theme of joy, no one was sure how it would be received. That thousands attend each conference with thousands more in overflow rooms and yet more on waiting lists is astounding to us.

Women obviously are hungry to come together en masse to worship, laugh, and be challenged to recognize that in Jesus Christ there is tremendous joy. Those of us on the platform are gratified to look out into the faces of women laughing so hard they can hardly stay in their seats and then listening with equal intensity as their faith is encouraged to flourish in the knowledge of who God is. The letters that pour in after each conference detailing the life-changing and restorative power of these women's experiences are indicative of God's presence. Were it not for his healing touch we would merely be having fun, and the impact would be short-lived.

I love Psalm 90:14; it validates God's intention for each of us. "O satisfy us in the morning with Thy lovingkindness, that we may sing for joy and be glad all our days" (NASB).

In addition to the unexpected joy curves are those wonderful curves that feed my senses. By that, I mean those times when I am literally on the road traveling, round a curve, and come upon a scene so spectacular I could cry.

For instance, I can't drive through the Rocky Mountains of Colorado without going into sensory overload. I remember the time, many years ago, when my parents, my husband, Ken, our three-year-old, Jeff, and I were driving through Telluride. Our intention was to stop at Trout Lake for some fishing. Mom and I had packed a fabulous picnic. So, while Dad regaled Ken with his latest fish stories in the front seat, Jeff chatted animatedly with his grandma in the backseat. I sat beside them, my head stuck out the window.

There were a number of reasons for this. To begin with, I am prone to carsickness, and the bigger Dad's fish grew in his stories, the faster he drove. The road was curvy and a real challenge to the breakfast I had eaten several hours before, so this position seemed only practical. In addition, the Rocky Mountain air is piercingly clear, slightly pungent, and so characteristic of Colorado. I can never get enough of it. What better way to tank up than to hang out the window? Incidentally, I love seeing dogs happily riding in their masters' cars, their heads out the window. Though my ears may not flap in the wind, I relate.

As we gained altitude, the curves became even sharper, but mercifully Dad slowed down, and I pulled my head back into the car. When we rounded the last curve before the dirt road leading to Trout Lake, little Jeff leaped from his seat and shouted, "Grandpa, stop!" Directly in front of us were a mother deer and her two spotted fawns. We watched as they moved off the pavement and headed down an embankment to a gorgeous alpine meadow that only God could design. The deer seemed unconcerned with us, as with dignity and grace they entered the meadow and disappeared among the multitudinous colors of alpine flowers.

I don't want to put you in a coma here, but I just have to say that the Rocky Mountain system is one of the richest botanical regions in the world. The pink mountain hollyander, blue Rocky Mountain columbine, yellow alpine buttercups, pink and white calypso orchids, yellow and blue lupine all melting in a suffusion of color is astounding. What a moment and what a reward after all those curves.

As if that were not enough, a short way down the dirt road we rounded yet another curve and came upon the breathtaking beauty of Trout Lake. Rimmed by the jagged Rockies, the lake was so still and silvery it looked like a photograph. We were all silent for a moment, and then Jeff whispered, "Grandma, is this heaven?" Later, much later, when we realized the fish simply were not biting and would not be biting, we decided it definitely was not heaven. Still, that day will live forever in my memory for the exquisite food it provided to my senses and my soul. Of course, we endured a lot of curves before reaching that nurturing scene.

All curves have built in rewards, even those that seem to produce only tragedy. We all experience curves in our lives, the unexpected turns of events that leave us altered, sobered, and sometimes questioning God's love for us.

When one is young, in good health and eager for life, it's hard to imagine that one's experience could turn tragic or unfair. And yet, if we live long enough, that reality will crash through the picket fence sooner or later. And sometimes the curves are very sharp indeed.

Ken and I got married when I had just turned twenty-two and he twenty-three. We felt very mature and eager to begin married life together. Ken was a tremendous planner and was always mapping out events for us. I tend to go with the flow and like spontaneity. However, at that time I felt Ken's way was usually preferable, and I would generally defer to him.

I was to teach for two or three years (I lobbied for the "or"), and then we would have children. The first would be a boy. Two years later we would have another baby—a girl. That would complete the family. I asked if we could slip a dog into the plan. It was considered, and we ended up with three. Ken would teach, go to graduate school, earn a doctorate, and ultimately become one of Orange County's youngest superintendents of schools.

True to plan, two years after we were married, we had a baby, a boy. Two years later, true to plan, we had another baby, a girl. While still in the delivery room I thought, *Ken Meberg, you are incredible. Your gift for planning is truly impressive!*

But my euphoria after the effortless birth of little Joanie was short-lived. There was a problem, the doctor tried to explain to us, and it was serious. Joanie was born with spina bifida, a defect of the spine in which part of the spinal cord and spinal fluid are exposed through a gap in the backbone. This defect was more life-threatening in the sixties than it is now. At best, her life would be characterized by many operations and hospital stays but never normal living.

I really couldn't grasp what Dr. Webster was saying. I'd never heard of spina bifida, and besides, it wasn't in the plan. I told him to talk to Ken Meberg. There wasn't anything he couldn't take care of.

I soon realized this was beyond even Ken's abilities. I was twenty-six years old and had just experienced my first sharp curve on this journey through life. All the planning in the world couldn't prevent its devastating impact.

Ken's father had died when Ken was twelve, so this was not his first sharp curve. However, that curve hadn't prepared him for this one. It's an odd thing about sharp curves: Somehow they always catch us flat-footed, unprepared, and surprised no matter how many times we've been around the bend already.

In an effort to cope we devised yet another plan. We decided that God intended to do a miracle with little Joanie, primarily for the sake of the women in my neighborhood. You see, I had reluctantly started a Bible study six months prior to Joanie's birth. These women were utter pagans, disdainful of our faith, their lifestyles out of sync with ours. And I was sure they didn't like me. Yet I had sensed God wanted me to start this Bible study, so I had done so. I announced that I would teach the book of Mark in my home every Tuesday morning. I could courageously make this announcement because I truly believed no one would come.

But they came, all ten of them. And within a few months, all prayed to receive Christ as Savior. I was astounded. God was working. So now maybe it was his plan to continue his work by healing little Joanie's body for the sake of buoying the faith of these ten baby Christians.

Ken and I were, of course, familiar with Isaiah 55:8, which reminds us that God's ways are not our ways, neither are his thoughts our thoughts. But we couldn't believe this would not be "his way." It would make so much sense.

Then, on the fifteenth day of her life, we encountered another even sharper curve. Joanie died of spinal meningitis, a complication from her spina bifida. She had never come home from the hospital. I had never even held her in my arms.

Somehow we got through the days and weeks that followed. Ken immersed himself in his doctoral studies, while I set about trying to make sense of it all. That's what I frequently try to do with really sharp curves. If I can just figure out why it happened, how I could possibly have prevented it, or at least what satisfying theological label I can attach to it, then maybe I can come to terms with it. But this kind of strategy is an attempt to do the impossible.

Life often doesn't make sense; God often doesn't make sense. In this situation, what did make sense was the reward that was mine after maneuvering the sharp curve. I'll never be the same.

One morning, a number of months after Joanie died, I sat in my bedroom with my Bible on my lap. I love the Psalms and frequently meander around in them; sometimes with a specific purpose but often just because I like going there. On this particular morning, I found myself in Psalm 62.

I was reading along with some measure of indifference until I came to verse 11: "One thing God has spoken, two things have I heard: that you, O God, are strong, and that you, O Lord, are loving" (NIV).

Whoa! "That you, O God, are strong." Yes, strong enough to have healed Joanie . . . but you didn't. Strong enough to have prevented the defect in the first place . . . but you didn't. Strong enough to heal any of your children . . . sometimes you do and sometimes you don't. All of this I do not understand.

This was a crossroads on my journey: I could rail against God for what he did and did not do. I could be bitter, lose my faith, or more realistically, just become a whiner. On the other hand, I could heed the following phrase, "You, O Lord, are loving."

As a preacher's kid, I was taught biblical truths both at home and in church. One of the foundational truths I heard over and over was that Jesus loved me. It was the first song I ever learned to sing. And now, it was as if the message "Jesus loves me" that started in my youth had gathered snowball momentum until it literally rolled all over me that morning. "You, O Lord, are loving."

What a liberating truth! I do not now nor will I ever have all the answers for my many imponderable questions about God. But that morning he rewarded me with the sweet knowledge of his love in a way I had not previously experienced. It softened me, it satisfied me, and it served as a salve for my bleeding soul.

In spite of that pivotal experience, I still frequently need to be reminded of the truth of God's love. This assurance is crucial as I ride out the curves on my journey. If I'm unsure of his love, I tend to either think the curves are clear evidence that I'm not one of the favored ones or that he wants to use the curves to punish me for something.

But life is simply full of curves—sometimes gentle, pleasant, and surprisingly gratifying and sometimes threatening to over-whelm me in their sharpness. The seat belt insuring my survival is that one profound and simple truth: Jesus loves me.

I've buckled up with one of my favorite Scripture passages many times. Maybe it will help you feel secure, too. "We need have no fear of someone who loves us perfectly; his perfect love for us eliminates all dread of what he might do to us. If we are afraid, it is for fear of what he might do to us, and shows that we are not fully convinced that he really loves us. So you see, our love for him comes as a result of his loving us first" (1 John 4:18–19 TLB).

So when the road sign Curves Ahead pops up in your life, tighten the seat belt of his love and remember he is strong and capable of using that strength on your behalf—sometimes in the most amazing ways.

Three

Drive Friendly

Luci Swindoll

> "Toto, I've a feeling we're not in Kansas anymore."
> —DOROTHY, *WIZARD OF OZ*

Pull to the right, Mary. You're clipping hedges over here. Please pull over. I think I've lost my left kidney out in these weeds someplace."

"I can't just *pull over*, Luci. Don't you see the oncoming traffic headed straight for us? Better to wind up in the ditch than run into somebody."

"Are you *crazy*, woman?! It's *I* who will be in the ditch if you don't pull over."

Those were the words my friend and I yelled at each other on an otherwise pleasant summer's day as we were driving through the Cotswolds in jolly old England. Ever try to drive in England? Well, let me tell you, it's an undertaking like no other. Opposite side of the road, opposite side of the car, shifting on the opposite side of the steering wheel ... all that and more. The oncoming motorist knows not that you know not what to do, and you want to appear confident, so you plow ahead. As does he. It's sort of a European version of "chicken"; who will pull into the ditch first?

We had started out on this leg of our vacation with good intentions and heretofore had had a marvelous time—laughing, singing, eating—loving our days together in France and England. But something about getting into a car can turn normally sane people into crazed maniacs. The phrase, "Drive Friendly," which appears on road signs in Texas, is largely forgotten when one climbs into a vehicle.

We had decided to spend two or three days in the Cotswolds before catching a train into London, and so had rented a little car in Oxford, a four-door Korean model called a Daewoo, an innocent enough name. In fact, it sounded like baby talk to me, and I liked that. Our "Little Baby Daewoo," we affectionately called it.

Mary had designated herself the driver because she had been to England before and had ridden these same roads with another friend. (I found out later the other friend had done all the driving.)

Even as we were leaving Oxford to go to Woodstock Oust, a thirty-minute drive up the road, we encountered trouble. Right in the heart of downtown Oxford we turned the wrong way on a one-way street and were immediately pulled over by a bobby. We hurriedly confessed to him the obvious: We don't know where we are; we didn't mean to do it and so don't deserve a ticket; we're here on holiday; the car is rented ... As we were mouthing on and on, he waved his hand and, in the kindest manner of a stately gentleman, began to apologize for the one-way street and to explain that he knew it was inconvenient and rather archaic even for old Oxford. "I say, this should have been changed into a two-way street years ago," he said.

He told us how to extricate ourselves from the maze of streets and crowds of people. Pointing this way and that, he was ever so friendly. He even drew us a map that we momentarily treasured but soon found utterly ineffectual. As we followed our instincts, we eventually wormed our way out of town and, with fear and trembling, onto Highway A44 north toward Woodstock.

I was grateful when the driving was finally over for the day and we were settled into a lovely evening at The Feathers, a privately owned and operated seventeenth-century hotel where Mary had stayed before.

On the second day (the day of our yelling spree), we determined we would make a circle through the Cotswolds in Little Baby Daewoo, and as Mary drove, I would take pictures. And so, with our assigned duties, we cheerfully started out. Talk about road signs, the British have some that are worth noting: Kill Your Speed was one we decided we didn't want to fool with and Dead Slow could not be misunderstood. Since we never saw the sign, Drive Friendly, I suppose we thought we didn't have to do *that*. We just tootled along: Blenheim Palace first, then Chipping Norton. From there to Moreton-in-Marsh, Stow-on-the-Wold, Upper and Lower Slaughter . . . all those charming and adorable towns one could get lost in and be content forever.

I've always been somewhat amused at the names of these fascinating places, with the preposition in the middle of the name: Stratford-upon-Avon, Ascott-under-Wychwood, Burton-on-the-Water, Clapton-on-the-Hill, and so forth. At the moment I was convinced we were about to mark a new area: Girl-in-the-Ditch.

When long shadows began to swallow up the sun, we started our drive back to Woodstock. This was when our verbal exchange first started. It was kind at first. "Mary, honey, watch it. I know you didn't mean to, but you just hit the curb."

"Oh, I'm sorry, Luci. It's just that the traffic is so heavy, and there's a string of cars behind me, wanting to pass."

With a couple more miles of road behind us, my voice began to rise. "Gosh, do you want to kill us both?! Pull over to the right. Let me drive!"

"Calm down, Luci," Mary fumed. "You can't imagine how hard this is. Everything is backward."

The tension grew as horns began honking behind us, impatiently prodding us to go faster, while oncoming cars blinked their lights at us to get out of their lane. All the while we were gesturing wildly at one another, trying to make our respective points.

Finally Mary yelled, "Lord, will you please give me your comfort? Please. This is so hard, Lord. I have a knot in my stomach, a pain in my neck, a headache, and such tightness in my chest I can hardly breathe. I am *not* having a fun vacation. Show me you are with me, Father, would you please?"

I decided to shut up as it's kind of hard to yell at somebody who is praying. Mary looked over into a field of high grass then and hollered, "Look! Look at that sign. It says 'Jesus Cares.' Can you believe it? There's my comfort. All right!"

We gave each other a high five and laughed at the Lord's ingenuity. It was only when we got a little closer that I realized the sign didn't say "Jesus Cares" at all but rather, "Jersey Cream." Some farmer in the Cotswolds was advertising his dairy products to passersby.

Mary and I have laughed many times as we've remembered this moment. She insists that even though it was only *perceived* encouragement, it was exactly what she needed to get us safely to the hotel. It certainly was just the reminder I needed: Jesus does care about us—our needs, our troubles, our fears, even our loss of temper. Never mind that I marched right up to our room, picked up the phone, dialed the bar, and ordered the stiffest Perrier in the place. Between that and a hot bubble bath I knew I was going to live and that Girl-in-the-Ditch was nothing more than a clipped hedge and a chipped curb somewhere between the quaint towns of Minster Lovell and Woodstock.

You may have never driven in the Cotswolds or had to deal with a car in which all the driving mechanisms are opposite from what you're used to, but I'll bet my last nickel you have been riding along with somebody and wanted to bite her head off—whether Jesus cared or not. And this wanting to bite someone's head off doesn't just happen in cars; it happens in life. We've had it up to here with somebody, and the only thing we want to do is *tell her off*. The concept Drive Friendly seems like a joke.

Our lives are filled with tension. Many of us live in the fast lane with tempers right on the edge of our skin or at the end of our tongues, ready to be spewed out at anybody who looks at us the wrong way. The newspapers are replete with tension-producing articles and happenings that make us mad or fearful. Family differences and misunderstandings make for hard feelings and rude, hurtful exchanges, if not knockdown drag-outs. And I'm not naive enough to believe we can overcome this kind of tension with a smile through clenched teeth or repeating to ourselves one hundred times, "I won't act this way anymore." Deep and complex problems beset us and can soon overwhelm us. I know that.

How then can we become more aware of the way we treat other people? What has happened to the art of good, old-fashioned kindness? Why don't we drive more friendly down the road of life?

First of all, we must recognize that none of us are above unkindness. It doesn't matter if one is a non-Christian or has enjoyed a relationship with the Lord the majority of one's life. My traveling companion and dear friend Mary and I are both believers in Jesus Christ; we have loved him and served him since our teenage years. Yet we still became upset with each other that day in the Cotswolds. We let each other have it verbally.

Generally speaking, although we differ on many issues, Mary and I get along beautifully. Because we love and respect each other we try our best to avoid arguing, which is my second suggestion on how to Drive Friendly in relationships. We practice kindness on each other, and we are each learning to share our feelings and preferences without being unkind or unfriendly to the other.

Don't let me kid you; kindness takes work, and sometimes it takes keeping our mouths shut when we would much rather express our absolutely correct, flawless, and perfect points of view. Since we are aware that becoming upset is a real possibility, we try to practice what brings peace. All the while, we know that just because we are friends, we are not beyond speaking or acting unkindly.

My third point in driving friendly is not only to recognize that anyone can lose his or her cool with the slightest provocation but also that we must give each other a little space to blow off steam without blowing our stack in return. We can learn to let our loved ones have a little fit without thinking, *I'm fed up; this friendship is over.* It's comforting to know that we *can* blow off steam with our loved one (or even toward our loved one) without losing face or place with that person. This knowledge assures us that it's okay to feel our pain or tension.

My fourth tip in driving friendly is a technique that helps me handle those otherwise firecracker situations. I look for a window of relief, a possible laugh or two. I try to have a good time with whatever is causing the tension, to make a little game out of it. Try it. It will help you drive a little friendlier through life.

Last spring Marilyn and I were invited to speak at the same meeting on Mackinac Island, off the Great Lakes coast of Michigan. It was a delightful weekend. We had gorgeous accommodations in the Grand Hotel, three delicious meals a day, and meetings that were gratifying to both our souls and spirits. Afterward, we were told we need not leave the afternoon the conference ended but could fly to Pellston on the mainland in a little four-seater plane the next morning to catch our 7 A.M. flight to Detroit. This sounded wonderful to us. We had come to Mackinac Island on this little plane, loved it, and thought it would be fun to go back that way. Besides, that would free us for one night; we could relax and hang around in the hotel in our blue jeans and sweatshirts after all the conferees were gone. Good idea. We stayed.

Our hostess did warn us of one possible glitch; if it was foggy the next morning, the little plane would not fly and we would need to go by boat to the mainland—if the boat were running. We weren't worried. "How could it be foggy tomorrow morning," we reasoned, "when today is so absolutely, off-the-scale beautiful? Not a cloud in the sky."

Our wake-up call at 4:45 A.M. found us already up and almost packed. But when we went down to the lobby, we learned that the fog was so thick the pilot not only couldn't take us when we needed to go, but it was doubtful we would get out at all that day.

We had two choices. First, we could stew and fret because we didn't take the plane the previous evening. This choice would no doubt include getting mad and casting blame on one other, then becoming upset with the hotel's desk clerk for not warning us more strongly—or for letting it get foggy. Or, second, we could make a little game out of it. We decided to Drive Friendly.

Because no cars are allowed on the island, we had to hire a horse and buggy to transport us at pre-dawn on that cold (46 degrees) morning to the dock where we caught our waiting boat—motorboat—a kind of low-slung fishing craft. Because our driver was going to literally skim the top of the water as fast as he could go, we were asked to cram ourselves into the tiny enclosed area under the hull, already filled with life jackets. Laughing, we did so, remaining in a scrunched up position for the forty-five-minute dash through that narrow section of Lake Huron.

Upon docking, we unfolded our bodies, exited the boat, and raced, luggage in hand, to a taxi with its motor running so we could tear out to Pellston the minute we arrived. An hour and a half later, we pulled into the Pellston airport with thirty minutes to spare for the Detroit flight.

Not one harsh word was spoken by Marilyn or me from the minute we got up at 4:45 A.M. until we arrived home eleven hours later. In fact, we made outrageous bets along the way and had a hilarious time. Was it because we love to live on the edge and didn't feel any anxiety or disappointment? I don't think so. I believe it was because we chose to practice kindness and to do the best we could with a less-than-perfect situation.

As I have grown older, I've traveled a bit, and have often stayed for days at a time in the homes of my brothers, as well as in the homes of various friends. One of the things I enjoy most during these visits is the spirit of appreciation I see among family members. So often, all too often, we take each other for granted. In effect we say, "I live with him so I don't need to express thanks for every little thing." Oh, yes we do. When we live closely with others or spend a great deal of time with them, we need to remember that everything they do for us takes time and energy they could be using doing something for themselves or someone else. They should be thanked for that time. I'm talking about when they do simple, everyday things like making a bed, fixing a meal, or taking out the trash. To express our appreciation to our loved ones is to live in the spirit of love and harmony with them.

I don't know that I have ever seen either of my brothers get up from a meal his wife has prepared without expressing thanks for that meal. I really appreciate that. My dad started the custom many years ago, and now my brothers practice it in their homes. It's refreshing to be the recipient of kind words like "Thank you," "I'm sorry," or "I was wrong. Will you forgive me?"

Unfortunately, I haven't seen the road sign Drive Friendly anywhere but in my state of Texas. It would certainly be nice if every other state in the Union were to post it, as well. Just a little sign on the roadside to remind us to think about others, like the Jersey Cream sign reminded Mary and me a couple of summers ago that Jesus cares about us.

Mary told me she is friends with a couple who have been married for twenty-five years and who recently realized that some of the joy and sweetness had gone out of their lives together. With this in mind, they decided to fast from sweets and desserts for forty days and pray that the Lord would return to them the sweetness of his presence and that this sweetness would splash over into their marriage.

They knew they didn't want to live in complacency the rest of their lives, so they made up their minds to do something about the loss of kindness and sweetness in their relationship. It worked. They told Mary their marriage is sweeter now than ever before.

Have you ever noticed this encouraging little verse, "He who loves a pure heart and whose speech is gracious will have the king for his friend" (Prov. 22:11 NIV)? I want the hallmarks of purity and graciousness in my life—road signs to live by.

In Psalm 18:50 we are told that the Lord "shows unfailing kindness to his anointed" (NIV). Aren't you glad God is sweet to us, that he goes the extra mile to be kind even when we are undeserving?

His constancy should cause us to want to express our love and appreciation to others in gracious words and acts every day. Loneliness and isolation abound in the world, right in our neighborhoods, perhaps in our own homes. We all carry secrets—painful secrets that make us feel scared, alone, and sometimes alienated. If we knew how many secret feelings of pain resided in our own household, we would be amazed. Just being human means we often feel solitary or even rootless at the core of our being.

Charles Dickens says it poignantly:

> Every human creature is constituted to be that profound secret and mystery to every other. A solemn consideration, when I enter a great city by night, that every one of those darkly clustered houses encloses its own secret; that every beating heart in the hundreds of thousands of breasts there, is, in some of its imaginings, a secret to the heart nearest it!"[1]

---

[1]Charles Dickens, A *Tale of Two Cities* (Norwalk, Conn.: The Easton Press, 1981), 22.

Before I run the risk of being misunderstood, let me say that I do not believe we can humanly alleviate loneliness nor crank out friendliness, kindness, or sweetness day after day after day. Unless it comes through the power of God's indwelling Spirit, our attempts will fall flat, we'll get tired of cranking, and we'll give up. But knowing Jesus cares for us with an infinite amount of love and is willing, ready, and able to receive all our cares, we can ask him to give us his ability to practice kindness and graciousness with others. A personal relationship with God, through faith in his Son, Jesus Christ, puts us in touch with the supernatural power to greet people on the freeway with a smile instead of a frown. He reminds us to say "Thank you" and "Excuse me" to folks we often take for granted. He empowers us to keep our mouths shut when we would rather tell somebody off. He gives us the patience to let our friend blow off steam without setting fire to and burning down our otherwise wonderful relationship. In short, because Jesus cares, we care, too.

As I travel down the road of life with these crazy, exciting, adventuresome women on the Joyful Journey team, I am so thankful that we have all become such close friends. I thought of us the other day as I was listening to my old record, *The Wiz*, a play written and performed about twenty years ago. The cast of this musical version of *The Wizard of Oz* cuts loose on songs that remind us we can do anything in life if we use our heads, act with courage, and have a heart.

One of the numbers would make a great theme song for the Joyful Journey team. It's called "Ease on Down the Road," and it invites us to lay down our heavy loads and learn how to smile.

So, when it comes to your own joyful journey, remember to drive friendly and just ease on down the road.

 Four

No Outlet

Barbara Johnson

It is good to have an end to journey toward; but it is the journey that matters, in the end.
—Ursula K. Le Guin

My sister and I experienced the meaning of the street sign No Outlet in an off-the-street, behind-the-barn scenario. We were country girls in our twenties and all dressed up with someplace to go (though I can't remember where). We had stopped at a farmhouse to visit friends on our way to the locale that required we be spiffed up. Our farm friends convinced us to take a look at their new little piglets before we left. So the two of us trooped down the path until, near the end, we came to the pigpen. We were hanging over the fence, admiring the piglets and giggling at their antics when suddenly, we heard loud snorting sounds behind us. It was Mama Pig. And she was mad. Snorting and puffing for all she was worth, she charged the fence.

We leapt off the fence and, skirts and petticoats whirling, rushed toward the barn, hoping to find an open door. But in front of the barn, the mud became thick and deep, and our high heels immediately sank into the muck. We turned around only to see Mama Pig viciously snorting and squealing and hot on our oozy trail.

We had no outlet, no place to go. The only door was on the other side of the big red barn. A barbed wire fence ran along either side of the building. We had two choices; we could either climb up the barbed wire or let ourselves be trapped against the barn's side, then wait to be gored—or whatever it is a mad mama pig does.

We left our shoes to sink in the mud and scrambled up the barbed wire fence, tearing our dresses in the process. Finally, the farmer drove up in his truck to rescue us while the pig stood there snorting in a most disagreeable manner.

No Outlet traumas are like that: They leave you scrambling for any possible option, whatever it will take to get you out of the situation. Finding a way of escape isn't easy and usually comes at a significant price.

Years later, I can look back on that experience and laugh, but most No Outlet experiences are anything but funny. Yours may involve parenting a handicapped child, suffering with a chronic illness, dealing with a crippling accident, trying to absorb the loss of a loved one, or feeling the shame of a spouse's abandonment.

No Outlet suggests being surrounded by a wall. Some walls fence out what we fear, but most walls fence us in with our fear and we feel desperate to escape. Phrases such as "I ran up against a wall" or "I hit an impasse" express our frustration when we can't find a way out of our uncomfortable or painful situation. When we slam against a wall, our hearts bleed and our egos sag.

Walls can differ in thickness and in height. But they all have one essential element—impenetrability. The ugliest walls are built of the stones of disappointment. We aim for love and find rejection instead. We gaze into the mirror only to see the ravages of time in the lines on our faces. We get cancer or lose our job. Our fondest dreams smash into the wall.

Sometimes God is the one who erects the walls in our lives, blocking our goals. Lamentations 3:9 says, "He hath inclosed my ways with hewn stone" (KJV).

Of course, we realize that life is often hard and that the sun never rises or sets on a flawless horizon. But even when we can't penetrate a wall, we must know that new and beautiful vistas lie beyond it and that there is a way through. We may be able to lift our sights, double our efforts, and emotionally scale the wall we have been unable to physically climb over. Or possibly we can lower our sights, dig deep into the dirt of humility, and burrow under the wall, bending lower so that we can come out higher. Or perhaps we can emotionally move around the wall, reaching the green lawn later, but with our joy undimmed. No matter how high or ugly the barrier is, as long as we hold to the image of the green grass beyond the wall, we won't be permanently fenced in.

For many years, during freeway construction in our area of Los Angeles, a huge on-ramp jutted high into the air and then suddenly stopped. At the end of this ramp sat a number of large cement blocks to stop anyone who had ignored the No Outlet signs from plummeting to his or her death. That ramp was a chilling reminder that we should take signs seriously. When we find ourselves facing a No Outlet sign, we would do well to heed the warning and look to the Father for help.

No Outlet situations occur when our ordinary coping mechanisms and road maps fail. The purpose of these dead ends is not to trap us or depress us but to strengthen us.

If joy were the only emotion God intended us to feel, he could just zap us and take us to heaven right now. Instead, we are left facing a No Outlet sign. At such moments God offers strength so that we won't give in to despair, but be salt in the world, ministering to those around us who are hurting, too. No Outlet situations keep us in touch with life's harsh realities.

We can learn to *live* with difficult circumstances. Grace has the power to turn a seeming dead end into a new beginning, one that sets us on the path to life without end, amen. It is in that divine moment when grace breaks through the impossible situation and sets us emotionally free that we grow in our love for God. The reality of eternity is painted against the backdrop of our broken, hurting lives.

Sometimes, while traveling on life's journey, we get stopped by a bad attitude or by sin, which can cripple us. It's like having a flat tire that needs changing before we can continue on the road. With our destination firmly in our minds, we must first pull over and admit that something in our lives needs to change. Then we must jack the wheel off the ground and lift that situation to God in prayer. After that we must remove the flat tire and replace it with a new one, substituting the wrong attitude with a positive one. This new attitude can come as we meditate on Scripture and on the goodness of the Lord. A favorite verse that aids my venture back onto the road is Philippians 4:8: "Whatever is true, whatever is noble, whatever is right, whatever is pure, whatever is lovely, whatever is admirable—if anything is excellent or praiseworthy—think about such things" (NIV). Then we must lower the car and get ready to put that new attitude into practice. Finally, we can start the engine and get moving once again. Back on the road, try humming these words in your head: "Commit thy way unto the Lord ... and he shall bring it to pass" (Ps. 37:5 KJV).

When we make a commitment to fill our hearts with thoughts of his grace and power, the breath of God can inflate our flattened view of life. The word *encourage* means "to fill the heart." Encouragement can actually inflate a deflated attitude because it fills us with hope.

What is hope? It is the conviction that, despite all the black around you, despite the fact that you see no sign of an exit, you will find a way out—with God's help.

But it can seem like an eternity before we find a way out from under our problems. The word *eternity* is used only once in the Bible—in Isaiah 57:15: "For thus saith the high and lofty One that inhabiteth eternity, whose name is Holy; I dwell in the high and holy place, with him also that is of a contrite and humble spirit, to revive the spirit of the humble, and to revive the heart of the contrite ones" (KJV).

Yet we know that a seeming eternity can be many things. Waiting for a tow truck to show up, for a freeway exit to appear when we are headed in the wrong direction, for the light to turn green when we have spotted an empty parking space across the intersection. For a child's fever to break. For the pain to end.

As Christians, we anticipate that we will spend eternity in glory with God. But the trials of this present world often make us feel trapped in the nasty now. The sweet by-and-by seems more and more like a fantasy.

The events of our lives, when we let God use them, become the mysterious and perfect preparation for the work he has called us to. The truth is that our trials are a furnace forging us into gold.

Sometimes we wonder if we will ever emerge from a No Outlet situation. And yes, it may take a while for life to get back to "normal," whatever that is. Robert Frost said he could sum up everything he had learned about life in three words: "It goes on." It's true—you may work hard and finally arrive on Easy Street, only to discover there is no parking.

Fortunately, in Christ we have a love that can never be fathomed, a life that can never die, a joy that can never be diminished, a hope that can never be disappointed, a purity that can never be defiled, and resources that can never be exhausted.

When we talk about getting trapped on a No Outlet road, I think of the phrase "live it up" because *up* is one way *out* of a No Outlet place . . . up and over the wall, remember? Now, to most of us, "living it up" means living high, wide, and handsome. But the dictionary tells us that the adverb *up* means from a lower position to a higher position, in a state of being prepared, or in a state of completion or perfection.

So why not *live it up* for God? We can also *wake up*, for the night is coming. Then we can *cheer up* because we have so much to be thankful for in our salvation. We also must *stand up* and be counted for Christ. Then there's the need to *give up*; we can't straddle the fence where God is concerned. We let go of the world so that Christ can provide us with things so much better, such as joy and peace. Then we can *build up*, growing in grace and in the knowledge of Christ. This building up requires food (the Bible), fresh air (prayer), and exercise (service). All the while it's a *hold up*; that is, Christ holds us up with his mighty hand. Finally, we will reach the glorious climax to this live-it-up life. Someday we will be *caught up*. Yes, right out of this dreary world into the realms of glory.

Recently I started collecting pictures and figures of the angel Gabriel blowing his horn, signifying the Lord's coming. So far I have several pieces displayed around my home. Each reminds me that one day the trumpet will sound, and I'll be out of here!

One thing we are *not* to do is *shut up*. We are to keep our mouths open in testimony for the Lord.

Try praying daily, "Lord, please let me live it up today." God understands that you want to live with your mind fixed *up*on him.

Romans 8:18 reminds us that heaven's delights will far outweigh earth's difficulties. In the Bible we read over and over what we can expect to receive in heaven. I love that. The anticipation of heaven helps me keep my perspective, reminding me that the sufferings of this present time are not worthy to be compared with the glory that will be revealed. Every No Outlet circumstance I have ever faced will pale when I see Jesus.

Someone once said that life is made up of the tender teens, the teachable twenties, the tireless thirties, the fiery forties, the fretful fifties, the serious sixties, the sacred seventies, the aching eighties ... shortening breath, death, sod, God. That is our journey, and a happy ending awaits us after we make our way through all the tough stuff.

I love the cartoon that shows Ziggy standing before an Exit sign hanging on a brick wall.

When life becomes especially hard and troubles seem to gang up on us, I have a few suggestions. First, don't struggle and fret and try to cope all by yourself. Put the situation in God's hands, trusting that he will bring it to the conclusion that is best for everyone involved.

Second, pray for guidance and believe that direction is being given to you *now*.

Third, pray for and practice a calm attitude. Disturbing events will keep on being disturbing as long as *you* are disturbed. But when you become peaceful, conditions iron themselves out. You can't think creatively when your mind is upset. Remember: upset minds upset, peaceful minds bring peace.

Fourth, let faith saturate your thoughts. Say Isaiah 26:3 aloud every day: "Thou wilt keep him in perfect peace, whose mind is stayed on thee" (KJV).

Fifth, remind yourself of one great truth: Hard experiences *do* pass. They will yield. So just hold on, with God's help.

Sixth, remember that there is always a light in the darkness. Believe that and look for it; it is the light of God's love. Psalm 119:105 says, "Thy word is a lamp unto my feet, and a light unto my path" (KJV). You can go into the darkness unafraid.

Seventh, ask the Lord to release your ingenuity, so that you can face the problem creatively with strength and wisdom.

Eighth, remember that others experience troubles similar to yours. Many years ago a graduating class gave a stone bench to their university on which was engraved these words: "To those who sit here sorrowing or rejoicing: Greetings. So also did we in our time."

Ninth and last, hold on to this great promise: "God is our refuge and strength, a very present help in trouble" (Ps. 46:1 KJV). This is the truth; God will see you through. He will provide a way out. The sun will shine again. "For what is seen is temporary, but what is unseen is eternal" (2 Cor. 4:18 NIV).

No Outlet signs are usually found on dead-end roads in the midst of quiet neighborhoods. Well, who wants to turn down a road whose end is death? Yet, death is one of the harsh No Outlets we humans face. As much as we would like to avoid the reality that life on earth must conclude in death, at some point we must reckon with it. Still, those who love Christ will be provided a way out of death too. Our departure from earth simply means our arrival in heaven.

In his book, *When Loved Ones Are Taken in Death*, Lehman Strauss wrote about a church he pastored in the eastern U.S. He and others from his congregation would regularly make the trip to New York to say farewell to missionaries leaving for the field. The church members would linger on the dock until the ship was almost out of sight. Invariably, someone would comment, "There they go!"

Lehman Strauss made this application:

> Now, no one would question that [the missionaries'] departure from New York meant that they would be arriving at some other place at some time. When we are absent from one place, we are present at another. Somewhere, sometime, someone will be heard saying, "Here they come." Likewise, when God calls our believing loved ones out of our midst, we say they have departed. In heaven they say, "Here they come." The dead are absent from their bodies and from us, but they are present with the Lord.[1]

[1]Lehman Strauss, *When Loved Ones Are Taken in Death* (Grand Rapids, Mich.: Zondervan, 1964), 25–26.

When our Christian loved ones are taken, with grieving hearts we bid them farewell. We will miss them. But we must remember that the saints in heaven rejoice as the newcomers arrive. Departure time here is arrival time there. I like to think of death as God's way of saying, "Your table is ready."

A cartoon I saw once showed a little boy and girl looking up into the sky and saying, "If you look real hard, right there, you can see Grandpa in heaven smiling and winking at us."

Thunder clouds many times bring showers of blessing. We wonder how such awful things can happen to good, dedicated Christians. At the same time, we know the righteous are not exempt from accident, sickness, and death. If they were, everyone would become a Christian—but for the wrong reason.

Of course, inexplicable moments do come in which God chooses to spare us. A few years ago, as I was driving down the freeway in the fast lane (where else?), I noticed I was quickly approaching my exit—Florence Avenue. I started to swerve across the lanes, when suddenly something told me to exit at Slauson rather than Florence. I argued with myself—why should I get off at Slauson when my regular exit was so simple and direct?

The feeling persisted, and so I crossed over three lanes to make the Slauson exit. As soon as I reached the bottom of the off-ramp, a tremendous roar and crash sounded behind me. Huge flames leapt up from the freeway. Smoke and fire were suddenly everywhere.

In seconds, an entire section of the Harbor Freeway was demolished. Many cars burst into flames, and concrete blew like cylinders around the Slauson ramp. I learned later that a gasoline truck had exploded, flooding thousands of gallons of gas onto the freeway. If I had not exited at the precise moment I did, my car would have been a direct target.

Was that God's voice I'd heard? Was he protecting me from danger? Was fate somehow involved? What about all the others whose lives were snuffed out at that moment?

I happen to believe God had his arm of protection around me for some purpose I may never understand. He protected me from a situation in which there truly would have been no way out. He alone knew what was best for me in that moment.

But such narrow escapes are unusual. More often than not, God seems to ask us to endure No Outlet traumas rather than escape them. Whether we are spared or not, I believe God wants us to accept the situation we are given with openness and humility.

Remember, difficulties are opportunities for growth. How can we grow with no problems? The world is watching how the Christian acts under pressure. So don't be a pressure-filled bottle, but allow God to make something out of your problem. If we can stop complaining, we can start proclaiming what God is doing through our difficulties. Find a support group. And remind yourself that after every Calvary comes an Easter.

I saw another cartoon where Ziggy is driving along and comes up to a sign that says, "Harsh Realities Next 2,500 miles." Isn't that the way life is?

Yet we know that whatever touches us has first passed through the hands of our heavenly Father. God never has to say "Oops." Whatever comes, he has already surveyed and approved. Our pain is no accident to him who guides our lives.

Our heavenly Father is committed to shaping us into his image, and so he knows the ultimate value of each painful experience. No Outlet traumas are not unique—to you or to this time in history. This road sign has marked everyone's path. God asks us to face these dead ends with an air of expectancy that his peace and power will prevail. And they will.

So, when you find yourself at those Red Sea places in your life, with no way out, remember—there is always a way through.

 **Five**

Private Road No Access

Patsy Clairmont

It is the final voyage into oneself that is the most difficult.
—Haki Madhubuti

Private Road No Access. Now this sign intrigues me. *Private* for me connotes something secretive. In fact, a secret that's so good, whoever has it doesn't want to share it. And "no access" lets me know that it's only by personal invitation one will ever uncover the mystery behind the privacy. It's not that I can't keep a secret; it's that I don't want one kept from me. That's why I find this Private Road sign rather, well, inviting.

I have had to learn boundaries, for I've always felt what's mine I'll gladly share and what's yours I'll also share. Like Marilyn's dessert. I take joy in dragging a sizable chunk off Marilyn's bread pudding with my fork and inserting it into my mouth. For some odd reason my friend isn't terribly fond of this pastime of mine. (I think it's because she was an only child, but don't tell her I said that. I've noticed that only children are more prone to dessert boundaries.) Realizing this is mildly troublesome to Marilyn and seeing the Private Road sign in her eyes when her dessert arrives, makes the drive down that lane all the more tantalizing.

My Mamaw (grandmother) used to refuse all desserts ... until they arrived at the table. Then she invariably would spoon off a corner of someone's dessert for herself. (See, Marilyn, I come by this honestly.) Mamaw also liked to pinch off morsels of biscuits from nearby plates for her eating enjoyment.

Mamaw's fetish for hijacking food off of other people's plates drove my mom wild. As a result, my mom has highly honed plate parameters. Do not, I repeat, do not move fingers or fork toward Mom's plate for any reason. Her quick staccato raps on your knuckles for infringing on her victuals will leave your vitals racing. When my mom stakes her Private Road sign, she means no access, buddy.

"Buddy" was the word my mom and my Aunt Pearl always tagged onto the end of a sentence they really meant. We family members knew when "buddy" was uttered we had better sit up and pay attention, that this was a sign we were bearin' down on someone's last nerve. It was as if we had put on our blinker to turn down their private road, and they were loadin' buckshot to reinforce their point, whatever it was. We would do well to scatter.

Isn't it interesting how we all seem to have our own road sign language? When we truly know someone, we are able to read the signs and respond accordingly. If we care for the person and value the relationship, we want to honor the sign. (Uh-oh, Marilyn, I'm starting to feel guilty.) Sometimes, though, there are some, in fact a lot of somes, who don't take these clearly posted signs seriously.

Les and I were with friends once cruising around looking at homes when the friend turned into a clearly marked private community. I immediately objected, but our friend insisted it would be okay. I continued to protest, which turned our secret tour into misery. Our friend surmised that the private signs were meant for the troublemakers, not us law-abiding folks. What an oxymoron—law abiders who ignore signs.

Actually, I was motivated to obey not because it was the law (even though that's important to me), but because I didn't want to be caught and thrown out. I hate rejection. (Keep that in mind, Marilyn.) I was as curious about seeing the homes as my friend, just not as bold.

Although bold has certainly been a regular stat on my personal resume. Ask anyone who has known me for, say, five minutes. They'll tell you. Ask the guy in the log house. Les, Jason, Marty, and I were driving down a highway on our vacation when we passed a lovely log home on top of a hill overlooking a lake. I convinced Les to turn around and go back. When we arrived at the top of the man's driveway, Les asked what my plans were. I told him I was going to knock on the man's door and ask if I could take a picture of the outside of his house. Les just shook his head.

I knocked, the man answered, I asked, he erupted. "I am so tired of people invading my privacy," he ranted, much to my embarrassment. "Day after day I find uninvited strangers circling my property and clicking their cameras. I open my curtains and find people gawking. I'm tired of it!"

"My goodness, that must be so frustrating," I exclaimed. I admitted that we had been insensitive. And I agreed that it would be disconcerting to have strangers milling about your property at will. He began to soften then and to converse with us. Soon he not only forgave my inappropriate boldness but also graciously invited my family and me into his home for a tour.

I have never done that again to anyone. My goal was to get a closer look at his house, but I didn't consider that it would cost him the precious gift of his privacy. So, while I got to see his home, I also learned a lesson: I need to harness my boldness and show more respect for others' private space.

I have loved being a public person. I enjoy the platform, and I love interacting with people. Yet, the need to post Private Road signs in my life has increased with the years. My reservoir of strength is shallow; I need restorative times. My hot flashes are frequent. My need for rest has multiplied into sporadic nap-ettes. But because I have an energetic style of speaking, those in my audience expect me to have unending stamina. They are often thrown by my sometimes laid-back demeanor offstage; I go from Tigger onstage to Eeyore offstage. Learning to live with my limitations and to separate myself at times from people is difficult but imperative. And even though I may resist doing it, afterward I experience a rapid return of strength, and I'm able to maintain my joy. Private Road signs are mandatory for stability, sanity, and keeping my sense of humor.

You may love doing something but find that for whatever reason (demanding schedule, health, priorities) you have to post a Private Road sign on that area. Maybe you're a grandma, but you're just not up to keeping the grandchildren as frequently as you once did. Maybe your outside job is infringing on your at-home happiness. You may have been a faithful church worker, but now you are wrung out and in need of replenishment.

Perhaps you've come to realize that posting a sign is imperative if you are to continue on your journey with any semblance of joy. However, instead of a sign that reads Private Road No Access, yours might say Private Road Limited Access. Or maybe what you really need is a gate.

Gates come in various widths, heights, and shapes, but they all have a similar purpose—to invite or to discourage entrance. There are gates for ships, factories, communities, zoos, theaters, homes, gardens (desserts?). There are gates to keep children out of mischief, thieves away from the loot, and dogs off the mail carrier's ankle. There are narrow gates for keeping crowds orderly and in a single file.

A few years ago Les reluctantly entered the Disneyland gates, single file, with me nudging him along from behind. It's not that he had anything against Mickey and the others, but he was uneasy about going with me, his "Goofy" wife. Neither of us cares for whiplash or spine twister rides. In fact, Les doesn't like any ride he's not driving. I, too, prefer Les driving so I can tell him how. Anyway, the kid in me loves some of the more childlike offerings in the park. This was Les's concern.

When I spotted the Alice in Wonderland ride, I immediately wanted to take a whirl on it. But I had to put a hammerlock on Les before he would agree to go with me. You see, the ride is shaped like, well, a teacup. I guess the image of a barrel-shaped, bearded, middle-aged man sitting in a teacup was disconcerting to Les. I assured him that no one would see him because, as soon as we sat down, the teacup would enter a cave. When we exited the cave, the ride would be over, and we would slip out of the cup and into the crowd. What I didn't know then (during the hammerlock) was that at one point in our Wonderland journey the teacup would exit the cave at a higher level (with greater crowd visibility) and stop before reentering the cave to complete the tour.

So a moment later there we were, on display at the top of the cave—Tweedle-dum and Tweedle-dee. The short moment we were exposed felt like hours as Les scowled and scrunched down in the teacup. And I felt like a teabag in hot water.

Les has never accompanied me through the Disneyland gates again. He said he would only go back to the park if he had an armed guard to protect him from my antics.

What was I talking about? Oh yes—gates.

Buckingham Palace has a gate *and* guards. The presence of armed guards tends to discourage any mischief, such as someone like myself might try. (I'll bet no one nibbles on Her Highness's bread pudding.) And so there is no way annoying salespeople and aggressive gawkers can meander into the Royal Family's private space. Can you imagine the queen sitting through, say, a vacuum cleaner demonstration? I want to giggle just thinking of it—the queen in her tiara cavorting about the palace with a Kirby in high gear. But no fear of that happening; her gate is latched, the guards are alert, and trespassers are held at bay.

Likewise, our president's abode is a place of fences, gates, and security. Not long ago a man attempted to bypass the gate by flying a plane into the yard of the White House. He smacked—splat—into the White House itself! That's a rather obnoxious way to crash a party, make a point, or gain the president's attention. The pilot went from the White House to the Big House, passing through a gate, a heavy one with a dead-bolt latch. Hmm, seems whether by land or air, gates impact our journey.

Much of my journey these last ten years has taken place in the friendly skies, which means I spend tons of time in airports. After checking my luggage (my newest suitcase is the same size as my living room), the next item of business is to find my gate number. Once informed, I make the gate my priority destination. When I arrive at my gate, I then check for two things—the rest rooms and the gift stores (wouldn't want to miss a shopping opportunity). When it's time to walk through the gate, I must have my permission slip (ticket) in hand and a designated seat. If I don't, I'm not allowed to enter the jetway.

Gates are what we need in relationships. People, generally speaking, should have permission (a ticket) to enter our lives and be seated. For not everyone is trustworthy.

Recently, a salesman, under a cloak of deception, made his way into our living room. Oh, all right, I admit it; I gave him permission. But as soon as we discovered his ploy, we immediately registered our disapproval and disinterest. We gave him many subtle hints that we were ready for him to leave, but he wasn't about to budge. Finally, we became extremely frank and physically ushered him out the door. I made sure to securely latch the gate behind him. It would be a cold day you know where before I'd be that gullible again . . . buddy.

The positive side of a bad experience is that it can be a severe yet effective teacher; we don't soon forget the kinds of lessons that cause us some discomfort while learning them. This kind of lesson could even motivate us to install a gate if we don't already have one. My mistake, the day the salesman came touting his wares, was leaving my gate wide open. It seemed to announce that all were welcome, when in truth, I usually am cautiously selective.

The gate principle can be applied to relationships of all kinds. Closed gates symbolize a Private Road sign to those who do not belong. A latched gate suggests one needs a ticket, a reservation, or an invitation before entering. Those who latch their gates do so for good reasons.

Not too long ago, my friend Carol and I were visiting our mutual friend, Lauren, who had just moved to Malibu. When she mentioned the names of some well-known people who lived on her lane, we decided we would mosey down the road to perchance catch a glimpse of a famous someone sunning, gardening, or such. But we were disappointed when we saw the high walls and the secured gates surrounding the homes. They were obviously put there to prevent curious people like ourselves from gaping. Carol and I tried to walk tall in case a fleeting glance allowed us a peek into their world. But, then, how tall can a five-foot person walk? (I was afraid Carol's carrying me piggyback might be too obvious.) I'm sure these celebrities had plenty of reasons for building fences and gates around their fortress, their family, and their solitude. (I wondered if they, too, had encountered the salesman from hell.) And surely, their gates were latched and locked to secure their privacy.

I remember the time after a weekend of speaking I sat leisurely at my gate at the airport chatting with my host and hostess. We had arrived early because the event had concluded ahead of schedule, and besides, I don't relish frantic, last-minute sprints to gates. Eventually, as the time for my departure neared and we hadn't yet been invited to board, I sauntered up to the desk to see if our plane was delayed. To my dismay, I was informed I was waiting at the wrong gate.

"Run!" the folks at the desk prompted. "Your plane is getting ready to leave."

I dashed to the correct gate only to spot my plane backing away from the jetway. I protested (in a loud whine) to the lady at the desk and anyone else willing to listen. I wanted her to flag the pilot back in and let me board. (Yes, yes, I realize that was unreasonable . . . now.) She assured me it was a full flight and someone else was already very comfy in my seat. I plopped down with a thud in a nearby chair, panting and pouting. I tried to figure out how I had missed my flight when I had arrived two hours early. I had enough time, I had a ticket, I had a reserved seat. But I was at the wrong gate.

Scripture speaks of right and wrong gates: "Enter by the narrow gate; for the gate is wide, and the way is broad that leads to destruction, and many are those who enter by it. For the gate is small, and the way is narrow that leads to life, and few are those who find it" (Matt. 7:13–14 NASB).

This tells me that what appears right, popular, and sanctioned by man, may not be approved by God. The gate may be open, the traffic may be heavy, the people may be convincing, but they are entering the wrong gate.

It isn't that God has posted a Private Road No Access sign. It's that few are willing to enter through the gate of Christ. The cost of relinquishment and obedience is too pricey for them.

Our community recently conducted a tour of exceptional homes. Many who wanted to see the homes didn't because they were unwilling to pay the entrance fee. They were interested but not enough to relinquish their fifteen dollars at the gate. What a shame—there is nothing like entering in . . .

Jesus is our gate, for he gives us entrance to the Father. The Holy Spirit then begins to post road signs (via Scripture, witnesses, promptings, etc.) to give us the guidance we need to stay on the road of righteousness. Now we have reason to celebrate, for no matter how unpopular our road, no matter how treacherous it becomes, we know we are not alone, and we have entered at the right (narrow) gate.

The psalmist David puts it this way, "Enter into his gates with thanksgiving, and into his courts with praise: be thankful unto him, and bless his name. For the LORD is good; his mercy is everlasting; and his truth endureth to all generations" (Ps.100:4–5 KJV).

Have you entered in through the narrow gate of Christ to abundant and eternal life? When you do, you are guaranteed to never walk alone in your journey. Christ will walk with you every step of the way. Even down Private Roads. He is not only the gate that leads you to the Father, but he is also the gate all must pass through who touch your life. For the Lord, in his mercy and wisdom, will examine both the good and the evil before it impacts you, and then He will use it all for your well-being and his glory. And that realization, dear sisters, will add to your joy.

 Six

Yield

Marilyn Meberg

I been a wanderin'
Early and late,
New York City
To the Golden Gate
An' it looks like
I'm never gonna cease my
Wanderin'.

—CARL SANDBURG

The road sign Yield frequently gives me a giggle. Perhaps it's because my husband, Ken, always said that the best way to deal with temptation was to yield to it.

So, when this sign pops up periodically, I have an imaginary conversation with it. "Really, are you telling me to pull over and have a chocolate-covered donut?" Or, if I see a yield sign close to my favorite department store: "So it's a great summer sale, huh? You think I ought to check it out? Well, okay." As you can see, responding to a Yield sign has its benefits.

You may be questioning Ken's theology, and so let me assure you he didn't really believe in yielding to temptation ... at least not regularly . . . only if it had to do with jamoca almond fudge ice cream.

Not only do I love the road sign Yield, I love the word itself. It has so many layers of meaning. For instance, it can connote a soft spirit of cooperation as one defers to the needs of another:

"It's your turn to proceed through the intersection. Please go ahead."

"Oh, really, thank you so much. I truly thought you arrived first. How very kind you are."

"Not at all. Have a wonderful day."

"Oh, and you, too!"

In a conversation where points of view differ and energy runs high, one could show a conciliatory spirit and yield the floor to another in spite of her opposing view. This is evidenced in the following dialogue:

"I know you are strongly opposed to facial hair on women, Blanche, and I'd like to give you a chance to state your opinion."

"Well, thank you, Bernadette, I greatly appreciate this opportunity to speak against the look of the extended eyebrow. There is, in my view, no aesthetic benefit to an unbroken line of bristly hair linking a woman's eyebrows."

"Well, now, of course, that is a valid point, but do you not think one could look upon the extended eyebrow as a symbol rather than just an eyebrow?"

"I suppose so, but I must admit your meaning is not yet clear to me. Would you mind explaining?"

"I'd be happy to. You see, the extended eyebrow, not subjected to the intrusiveness of tweezers, can represent an at-homeness with the self, a gentle embracing of all that is natural. Not only that, it can symbolize unbroken unity and oneness of purpose, thus be a source of encouragement to our fragmented society."

You see the level of civility that is possible as we yield to one another?

Moving away from these mildly moronic examples, let's look at one of the specific definitions of *yield*. The dictionary defines it as "not rigid or stiff."

Don't you love those folks who are not rigid or stiff in their schedules but rather spontaneous and flexible? In my view, nothing is more stultifying than the person who won't ever change her routine or schedule to do something previously unprogrammed. Rigid adherence to our calendars can possibly increase productivity, but at the expense of spontaneity and joy.

For example, yesterday I wandered into my kitchen at 6:30 A.M. to activate my "Mrs. Tea" machine for breakfast and noticed a human being sitting on my patio reading the paper (*my* paper as it turned out). I stopped dead in my tracks and then realized it was Luci. I threw open the slider door. "Hey, early bird, what are you doing nesting on my patio at 6:30 in the morning?" I asked.

She looked up at me with a smile. "You wanna go out for breakfast?"

I rapidly thought through my tightly scheduled day; I had planned to spend the morning writing (the very book you are reading) and then run some crucial errands in the afternoon. Going out for breakfast would definitely throw off my timing, but then Luci and I had just recently become neighbors. It's the first time in twelve years we have lived anywhere near each other. How nice to take time to enjoy her nearness. "Okay, let's go."

Moments later, we were chortling over the world's finest cinnamon rolls as Luci fawned over Peter Jennings and his memorable broadcast the previous evening. (Actually, I think she has a crush on Jennings, but that's just my private opinion.)

As I sat down at my desk an hour and a half later than I had planned, I felt only joy for the spontaneous intrusion into my well-ordered day. It was a no-big-deal experience, but by the same token it was softly pleasant and soul satisfying. Also, I always enjoy a good cinnamon roll.

I hope never to be enslaved to routine. It brings with it a measure of sterility.

A synonym for the word *yield* is "concede." This, too, is a word for which I have warm feelings. It reminds me of my childhood. My pastor father was always making bets with my mother (not for money but stuff), and invariably my mother would win. Just prior to her easy triumph, however, my father would say, "Okay, Elizabeth, do you concede?"

Rarely did my mother need to concede because rarely was she wrong. Now, I don't mean to imply a know-it-all superiority; it's just that she had an amazing capacity for storing all kinds of information.

For example, Dad asked her one time: "Elizabeth, who wrote that line, 'Because I could not stop for Death/He kindly stopped for me'? Wasn't that Robert Frost?"

"No, Jasper [yes, his name was Jasper], that line is Emily Dickinson's."

"I'm sure it's Robert Frost. Do you want to bet a piece of pie on it?"

"Of course."

"Do you want to concede now, or should I go to the trouble of looking it up?"

Mother did not concede, Dad looked it up, and Mom won. Dad, however, rarely paid off his bets. He said it would be inappropriate behavior for a minister. I don't know if my mother bought into that logic, but she never seemed concerned that Dad nearly always got off the hook.

I remember one particularly energetic exchange between my parents that culminated in the usual bet. Dad insisted the Danube was the longest river in Europe. Mother maintained the Volga was. Dad pounced on what he was sure would be an easy "concede" and bet my mother a full week of making the evening meals if he was wrong. He was, and he cheerfully prepared wonderful meals for a week. (I guess paying off that bet didn't seem inappropriate to his "man-of-the-cloth" mentality.)

I enjoy remembering these incidents because there was no rancor on the part of my parents. To this day I have fun with bets based on trivial pieces of information. (Talk to Luci about some of these bets. I am always stunned when I lose and she insists I pay up!)

My favorite memory, though, is of a bet my mother had to concede. My dad pastored small rural churches in the state of Washington. In one particular pastorate in the town of Amboy, Dad became friends with an irascible farmer in the area named Harry Hooper. Harry didn't like ministers and had no interest in church, but Dad's persistent visits and bantering conversational style produced in Harry a reluctant but genuine affinity for my father.

I loved being a part of some of these pastoral wooings because Harry had a huge farm with more animals than I had ever seen in my life. He also had a fabulous barn with a hayloft. His son, Harold, introduced me to one of life's most exhilarating experiences—leaping from the hayloft into the stored hay some thirty feet below. But, as Sherlock Holmes would say, "I digress"; back to the bet.

One typically dreary and rainy afternoon, I accompanied my dad on a quick "drop-in" to Harry's place. We found him in the barn with a sow who had given birth to nine little piglets the night before. Harry was holding one of them in his beefy, freckled hand. He told us he was going to have to kill the little piglet because the mother had stepped on it. Harry didn't expect the baby to live and wanted to put it out of its misery.

My six-year-old heart could not receive this kind of news so I quickly headed for the barn door. "Just a minute, Marilyn," I heard my father say, and then he turned to Harry and asked if he could hold the piglet.

I watched my dad lightly run his fingers over the little pink mass in his hand. "Harry, I think this piglet can live," he said. "Why don't you let me take it home?"

Harry broke into a bellow of derisive laughter. "Well, Preacher, that's the craziest idea I ever heard, but if you want it, you can have it."

I was thrilled at the prospect of nursing this little piglet back to health. Dad started to carefully put the baby in my hands, but then he stopped and, in typical Jasper-style, said, "Harry, let's make a deal. If the pig lives, you come to church at least twice."

Harry roared with laughter again. "Preacher, if you can get that pig to live," he said, "I'll come to church for a whole year!"

Dad wrapped the piglet in his handkerchief and placed it into my eager hands. Later, as we entered our kitchen, Dad called out, "Elizabeth, would you like to participate in the most exciting bet of your life?"

Mom entered the room smiling warmly. She was always charmed by his irrepressible enthusiasm and sometimes crazy ideas. She rose to the bait. Thus far, she had not noticed the pink lump packaged in my hands.

"I've come upon a great way to get Harry Hooper to come to church. All we have to do is raise one of his injured little piglets right here in the kitchen!"

Mother watched in stunned silence as my father darted about gathering a shoe box, then a light bulb that he wrapped in asbestos, and finally some paper he shredded in narrow little strips. After Piglet was settled in its new bed and Dad had explained in greater detail the deal he had made with Harry, my mother continued to look perplexed. "I still don't know what the bet is, Jasper. Is it whether or not I will allow a pig to be raised in my kitchen?"

"No, Elizabeth, it's whether or not I can keep this little creature alive. Harry says there's no way. What's your bet?"

Mother peered into the paper nest at the motionless piglet and moaned slightly. "Oh, Jasper, I don't think this little one stands a chance. This is one bet I think you'd better concede." She glanced at my anxious face and added, "But we'll all do everything we can to see that I lose."

With an eyedropper, we faithfully fed little Piglet some sort of food concoction my dad knew to use. To our amazement, gradually Piglet rallied, outgrew her box, and ultimately, to my mother's discomfort and my utter joy, Piglet started limping around the kitchen. Her right leg and hip had been so injured she had to drag them along behind her, but she didn't seem to notice.

When she was two months old, Dad triumphantly returned Piglet to Harry. Dad won big time on that bet. Not only did my mother concede, but Harry also attended church every Sunday from then on. Conceding can often mean quite a triumph.

Another compelling inference we find in the word *yield* is the promise of rest, the cessation of struggle. This was clearly illustrated for me the last time I visited my little grandson, Ian. (It is most troublesome to me that Ian's parents flagrantly live outside of God's will. It seems so obvious that God wills them to live closer to this grandma! How on earth can I effectively teach Ian bad habits if he lives eight hours away? By the time I see him again, he has forgotten all I taught him on my last visit.)

One afternoon, in the space of about fifteen minutes, little Ian became so frustrated over his inability to catch the cat, Mama's refusal to let him run into the street, and the garden hose that would not uncoil from the spool, he fell into a heap of angry wailing. (I hadn't even taught him this yet!)

Beth scooped him up as he arched his back, kicked, screamed, and resisted her with all his strength. She finally managed to sit down with him in the rocking chair. As she sang softly, he quieted, became interested in nursing, and in a matter of moments, his little body was relaxed, even limp in his mother's arms.

What a picture of resistance he had been; what a picture of repose he became as he yielded to his mama's loving ministrations. Then, as if this depiction of the rewards of yielding were not enough, he looked languidly over at me across the room and softly said, "Happy."

He had been saying this word for several weeks now, and it thrilled me to death. How wonderful that one of his first utterances was "happy" instead of "doo-doo" or something equally as silly. When Ian had first spoken the word *happy* in my presence several days before the rocker experience, I was curious to know if he associated the word with an object or whether it had personal meaning for him. I assumed neither because, after all, he was only fourteen months old. But when he said "happy" within the meaningful context of yielding to his mama's comfort, he confirmed my deeply held convictions: The child is a genius. I must make phone calls.

So often we kick and scream at the thought of yielding. We don't want to give up control. If we could just understand that yielding to a benevolent and trustworthy "other" can bring quietness, rest, and even happiness.

I have just returned from a four-day visit to my mother's only sister in Colorado. I have loved and adored my Aunt Florence from my earliest memory. As a child I knew she loved me softly, deeply, and consistently. She bought me presents, listened to me babble, laughed quietly at my clownlike antics, and called me her "little Marilyn." As I grew older, I came to understand why she spent hours sitting motionless in a chair staring at the floor, the deep lines in her face expressing her inner anguish—they reflected the diagnosis of schizophrenia ascribed to her in her early twenties. It has always pleased me enormously to see her face light up, if only for a moment, at my presence or at something I might say.

This trip was no exception. As I walked into the rest home where she now lives, eighty-four years old and nearly blind, her face briefly lit up in recognition. "Marilyn," she said in her gentle voice. I know her interior terrain is too blighted for much joy, but that brief moment was sweet. She didn't say "Marilyn" again.

In addition to wanting to see Aunt Florence and take her on little outings each day, I was eager for her to give me power of attorney. This would relieve her of the tension she experiences as she writes out her fairly substantial check each month to this semi-private and very nice rest home. In spite of her illness and reclusiveness, she has a brilliant mind and has always taken care of her own business. She has not been well enough to work so she has no social security or retirement pension. As a result, she is watching the money my grandfather left for her dwindle so quickly she is alarmed. She wants to return to her home so as not to spend her remaining money. She refuses to believe her frailty and near blindness are sufficient reasons to remain in the rest home.

I tried every form of creative reasoning to convince her she would feel much less stress if I took over her business. (She doesn't know this part, but I have a plan to keep her financially afoot. It will only work if I am taking care of her business.) Unfortunately, she is unable to yield to my good intentions and my enormous love for her. To do so would be to relax, to cease struggling, and to enter into a more peaceful state of mind. But since she can't bring herself to relinquish her business, I can't ease her tension.

It isn't just babies like Ian who resist yielding. And it isn't just those whose minds are tormented and distrustful. It's all of us who for various reasons can't or won't trust in the promise of rest that yielding offers.

When I find I am unable to yield a point or to yield to the spirit of Jesus, I ask myself: What am I holding on to? Why is it so difficult to simply yield, knowing full well that I will benefit from doing so?

Like nearly everything in life, our resistance is formulated in our will. Thankfully, Philippians 2:13 reminds me, "For God is at work in you, both to will and to work for his good pleasure" (RSV). If I were on my own down here, I'd more often than not will for myself a resisting, stubborn, and unyielding spirit. But he promises to work in me and in my will. Since in my humanness I have trouble letting go and yielding, I'm enormously comforted by this promise of his active work in my will.

I've stumbled onto a few steps that help me transition from resistance to yieldedness and then to rest. Perhaps they will benefit you as well.

As you know, many Scriptures invite us to rest in him—the reward for yielding. "Come to me, all you who are weary and burdened, and I will give you rest" (Matt. 11:28 NIV). In Psalm 37:7 we are encouraged to "Rest in the LORD" (KJV). I frequently take these two verses and simply luxuriate in them.

Then I remind myself of one of the reasons God sent Jesus to earth: "to give light to those who sit in darkness and the shadow of death" (Luke 1:79 NKJV). When I refuse to yield, I am refusing the light; I am sitting in darkness where there is no rest. My participation, then, is mandatory if I ever want to come out of the darkness and into the light that he provides.

Isaiah 26:3 states, "He will keep in perfect peace all those who trust in him, whose thoughts turn often to the Lord" (TLB). My job is to focus on him, to "turn often" to him. One way I focus on him is to simply repeat his name over and over. I'm not talking about a mindless chanting, but a purposeful and reverent speaking of his name, that name that is above all names (Phil. 2:9); that name that will cause every knee to bow and every tongue to confess (Phil. 2:10–11); that name that Jesus invited us to use because it has power (John 14:13).

Generally, it is at this point I find myself no longer arching my back and kicking against his ministrations. Somehow the invitation to rest and the sweet power of his name enable me to join my will to his, to become quiet, even limp in his arms. Out of the richness of that yieldedness and the restoration that follows, I am strengthened, loved, and encouraged. I find rest.

I have shared with you my love of the road sign Yield because I truly believe yielding gives us joy on this journey. If your perspective has been altered at all and you can playfully respond to its implications, you may be enriched by sidling up to this sign. At this point you are ready to enter into all that the yield-rest principle offers your soul. In fact, like Ian, you may now be able to freely and frequently say "happy."

 Seven

Limited Visibility Ahead

Barbara Johnson

Thou has seen nothing yet.
—Don Quixote

Recently, on a visit to the North Carolina mountains, I encountered a sign on the winding highway that read, Limited Visibility Ahead. This is a rare sign in California, where freeway expanses give spacious views (except for traffic tie-ups, of course—oh, yeah, and smog). But the phrase, Limited Visibility, caused me to recall an old song entitled "If We Could See Beyond Today":

> *If we could see, if we could know, we often say,*
> *but God in love a veil does throw across our way.*
> *We cannot see what lies before, and so we cling to Him the*
> *more.*
> *He leads us till this life is o'er, trust and obey.*

The idea of God's throwing a veil across our way touches me, doesn't it you? How wonderful that we don't have to know the future but can be assured that a veil separates us from the up-ahead. We only have to concern ourselves with the problems and circumstances of today, leaving tomorrow to him.

A friend of mine owns a dog who has her own way of throwing a veil on the future. When it's time for a visit to the vet, the dog has to be boosted into the car's backseat, where she immediately plants herself looking out the back window. My friend isn't sure if this gesture is the dog's way of expressing anger at her owner, avoiding what's up ahead, or showing her disorientation at the dizzying thought of the car's destination.

How many of us would turn our backs on the future if we could clearly see what it held? If I had known at age twenty-five that I would lose two sons and be estranged from a third, I think I would have immediately "resigned." But because our future is unknown, we just take a plateful of life at a time.

After all, yesterday is a canceled check, and tomorrow is only a promissory note. But today is cash. We have the vision for today, not tomorrow with its uncertainties and challenges. I recall reading that "It is the weight of the tomorrows that drives men mad."

Life isn't a destination but a journey, and so we all encounter unexpected curves, turning points, mountaintops, and valleys. We discover the best in ourselves as each event occurs and shapes us into who we are.

The trip can be a long one, but we can support each other on the way by loving, caring, and softening the blows. This concept was vividly illustrated for me when my husband, Bill, and I visited the Billy Graham Training Center in North Carolina (where we saw the Limited Visibility sign). During a tour of the fabulous grounds, we noticed that every window of the main building offered a magnificent view of the mountains with distinct levels of height, greenery, and shadings. One can see far and wide;

one can admire the greenery close up and at the same time view the varying heights of mountains in the distance.

The tour guide explained to us that in the planning stages of the building, the architects realized that each window would have a limited view unless measures were taken to insure that any trimming or cutting down of trees would be handled properly to protect it. A person known as a Vista Specialist was hired to make certain the trees and greenery showed off the view to best advantage—the shades of green would vary depending on the time of day. The result was overwhelmingly beautiful.

I had never heard of a Vista Specialist. But it occurred to me that God is a Vista Specialist to those of us who trust him. He is the one who knows our future and the paths we will take during our journey. He fine-tunes us and shapes our foliage so those who are watching can admire his handiwork in us. And we can be assured that, because of him, life will always offer us beautiful vistas.

Joe R. Barnett tells the story of an American traveler in Italy. He came upon a lumberjack who was a different kind of vision specialist. The American watched with curiosity as the man would occasionally jab his sharp hook into a log and remove it from among the others floating down a mountain stream. When the tourist asked the man why he did this, the lumberman replied, "The logs I let pass grew in a valley and were protected all their lives; their grain is coarse. The ones I've picked out grew high on the mountains. From the time they were sprouts and saplings they endured heavy winds so they grew strong with a fine, intricate grain. We save these for the choice work; they are too precious to use as plain lumber."

If you have some sorrow in your life, some distasteful task you have to perform, some heavy cross on your shoulders, it may be that God is preparing you for a high purpose. You might not see it now, but yours may be a choice work beyond the capacity of "plain lumber."

God can use us for tasks we never dreamed of after he has fine-tuned us and shaped our lives through the stress and pain we suffer. Valley experiences can be treasures, while mountaintop experiences, where we are buffeted by storms, can strengthen us.

So much of the joy in life depends on how we see things. If we could remember the perspective in this poem, we wouldn't worry about limited visibility:

> He is ahead of you . . . as your shepherd.
> He is behind you . . . as your rearguard.
> He is above you . . . as your covering.
> He is beneath you . . . as your foundation.
> He is beside you . . . as your friend.
> He is within you . . . as your life.

It seems that, regardless of our circumstances, joy comes to those of us who look for it. I once heard a story by G. W. Target about two men who shared a small hospital room. Both of them were seriously ill. One man was allowed to sit up briefly each afternoon to help drain the fluid from his lungs. His bed was next to the room's only window. The other man had to spend his hours flat on his back.

The men talked about their families, homes, and past vacations. Every afternoon when the man by the window would sit up, he would describe to his roommate all the wonderful things he could see outside the window. The man in the other bed began to live for those moments when his world would expand as he heard about the activity and color in the outside world.

The window overlooked a park with a lovely lake, the man by the window told his roommate. Ducks and swans played on the water while little children sailed their model boats. Lovers walked arm in arm, and colorful flowers bloomed everywhere. As the man by the window described all this in exquisite detail, the man in the other bed would close his eyes and imagine the picturesque scene.

One warm afternoon the man by the window described a parade passing by. Although the other man couldn't hear the band, he could see it in his mind's eye as it was vividly described to him.

Unexpectedly, a thought entered the prone man's mind. *Why should he have the pleasure of seeing everything while I never get to see anything?* It wasn't fair.

At first, the man felt ashamed of this thought. But as the days passed and he missed seeing more sights, his envy eroded into resentment and soon turned him sour. He began to brood, and he found himself unable to sleep. He should be the one by that window. It was his turn. This kind of thinking now controlled his every waking moment.

Late one night, as the envious man lay staring at the ceiling, the other fellow began to cough. He was choking on the fluid in his lungs. The bitter man watched in the dimly lit room as the struggling man tried to reach his call button; he never moved, never pushed his own call button. It took less than five minutes for the coughing to stop, along with the sound of breathing. There was only silence.

The following morning the day nurse arrived to bring water for the men's baths. When she found the lifeless body of the man by the window, she quietly called the hospital attendant to take him away.

As soon as it seemed appropriate, the remaining man asked if he could be moved next to the window. The nurse was happy to make the switch, and after settling him into his new bed, she left him alone.

Slowly, painfully, he propped himself up on one elbow to take his first look out the window. Finally he would have the joy of seeing it all for himself. He strained upward until, at last, the scene became visible.

A blank wall. Nothing but a blank wall.

True happiness does not come through a window. Nor is it a gift delivered to our door each morning. Our circumstances are not what make our lives complete. If we wait for life to get just right, we might never laugh again. The pursuit of happiness is to choose a positive attitude and express it. The real odyssey of discovery consists not in seeking new landscapes, but in seeing with new eyes.

We don't have to travel to faraway locations to find enriching experiences. They are all around us, in the sun glistening on a pond, in our children's laughter, in a friend's warm embrace. When we open our eyes to the beauty of our own world, we discover the richest landscape of all.

Another story vividly brings home this idea. The day had not started out well for a certain woman. She had overslept and was late for work. Then some things happened at the office that only contributed to her harried condition. By the time she reached the bus stop for her trip home, her stomach was tied in an intricate knot. As usual, the bus was late and packed, and she had to stand up. The bus started, stopped, turned left, then right, pushing and pulling her in all directions. The day wasn't improving even as it came to an end.

Then she heard a man's voice up front proclaim, "Beautiful day, isn't it?"

Because of the crowd she couldn't see the man, but he continued to comment on everything the bus passed that added to his joy: a church here, an ice cream store there, a baseball diamond here, a library there. The atmosphere in the bus grew immediately more carefree, as did the woman's heart. The man's enthusiasm was so winsome, the woman found herself smiling. When the bus reached the woman's stop, she worked her way through the crowd to the door. As she did so, she glanced at the "tour guide"—a plump man, wearing dark glasses and carrying a white cane. He was blind.

As she stepped off the bus, she realized the day's tensions had disappeared. God had sent a blind man to help her see that, though things go wrong sometimes, even with limited visibility, it's still a beautiful world.

As we journey through life, it isn't always the outer conditions—curves, fog, or even heavy storms—that limit our visibility. Sometimes we can't see what's happening around us because we are so caught up with ourselves.

Few people have clear enough sight to see their own faults. Conceit is a form of "I" strain that doctors can't cure. Yet, when it comes to spotting the faults of others, everybody seems to have 20–20 vision.

You know, many folks have an impairment, but it's not with vision or even with hearing. It's with focus. You arrive at an intersection, look both ways, and still drive into the path of an oncoming car. A family member or coworker speaks clearly to you, and yet later you can't remember what the person said.

This "concentration deficit" is even more crucial in spiritual matters. You might read a particular verse that plainly resolves a concern of yours. Yet the very next day you go through the same stress because you are unable to remember the solution.

Our daily prayer needs to include a request for focus and memory—with a protection clause that keeps Satan from stealing God's words from us. Make sure that "what you have heard [and seen] from the beginning remains in you" (1 John 2:24 NIV). A focused and retentive mind can significantly improve your sight, hearing, and contentment.

As one adage expresses it:

When the child of God
looks into the Word of God
and sees the Son of God
he is changed by the Spirit of God
in the image of God
for the glory of God.

The limits of our emotional visibility are all the more obvious when night comes and the brightness of day disappears. Trials weigh heavy on us as we lie down for the night. Our minds seem unable to bear the pressure, and we toss and turn. Somehow the darkness and aloneness make our problems seem all the heavier. Finally sleep does come, but only after hours of restlessness. Psalm 30:5 assures us, "Weeping may endure for a night, but joy comes in the morning" (NKJV). This is such a comfort when we are experiencing a dark night.

Sometimes God's mercy blows through our lives, and at other times it's the winds of adversity we feel. When cold winds of hardship make us feel restless, we can rest in God's promise that "joy will come in the morning." The iron crown of suffering always precedes the golden crown of glory, and God always places a time limit on the suffering of his children.

I saw a cartoon once that said, "Life generally looks better in the morning; it's just that morning takes so long to get here!" In the morning, things don't look as bad as they did several hours before. Why were we so overwhelmed and full of despair? What makes the difference? It's the joy that comes in the morning.

Not only are trials temporary, but they are also gifts from God. We can't deny that Christians are often called to endure soul-shaking experiences. In life there is weeping—and sometimes plenty of it. The nights of adversity are long and sometimes frequent, but God never allows them to be endless or without purpose.

One man who seemed to suffer a needless loss was Sir James Thornhill, who painted the ceiling of St. Paul's Cathedral in London. Because the rounded, vaulted ceiling is so high, Sir James had to complete his work standing on a scaffold several stories above the cathedral floor. One day when he had finished a particularly difficult part of the ceiling, he stopped to check his work. He began to move backward to get a better perspective. A helper working with him suddenly realized that if Sir James took one more step back, he would fall to his death. The worker also knew that if he shouted a warning, the artist might lose his balance. So, thinking fast, the helper grabbed a brush and stroked across the work Sir James was admiring. The artist instinctively moved forward toward his damaged work, and his life was saved.

No matter how drastic the action God takes in our lives, we can trust that he carefully weighs our trials. Relief may seem far away, but morning will come and with it God's promised joy. You have God's Word on it.

Of course, if you can find some humor in the situation, it will increase your joy. That happened to me the other day—over a couple of pillows, of all things.

I had dumped our old pillows in the trash. After several years, they had lost their newness and needed to be replaced. Bill had been reluctant to let go of his because he liked his bed pillow all squashed down—not fluffy or puffed up. He had clung like a child to his matted down, old pillow, which didn't puff up and look good.

In spite of all this, I bought two new pillows. They were terrific—big, fancy, blown-up jobs that looked really nice when the bed was made up, not sagging and squashed like the old, worn-out ones.

I was so happy. And then we laid our heads down on our new, very fluffy pillows, and immediately Bill began to complain that he couldn't sleep. The pillow was too hard and uncomfortable. I hated to admit it, since I was the one who had engineered this big transfer, but I felt a crimp in my neck as if I were sleeping on rocks. Maybe I had made a mistake replacing the old, soft pillows that had served us well for so many years with new stiff ones that refused to mold to our heads and necks.

After two nights of sleeplessness and listening to Bill's complaints, I knew I had to right the situation. I also knew where the old pillows were—buried in trash bags under a couple of days of accumulated litter.

Hurriedly I slipped on my housecoat and slippers and crept out to the curb where the trash bags were waiting for the garbage truck. Now, at 6 A.M. the sun was already up, and where we live lots of older people rise with the sun to go for morning walks. Plowing through our trash bags in public could earn me the title of "Neighborhood Bag Lady."

Desperately, I tried to undo the little twisties on one of the bags. Bill always fastened them so tightly.

After I finally opened the bag and dug around, I could see that the pillows weren't in this one. In my search, of course, I had spilled the bag's contents. Bill was so neat about how he collected trash, flattening every milk carton and cereal box and then tearing up the cardboard into tiny pieces. Recollecting all these tidbits and stuffing them back into the bag was quite a chore.

By this time, just as I'd expected, several couples had walked past me and nodded "Good morning." Knee-deep in trash, I simply smiled in return and kept digging. Finally I found both pillows. They were stained with grape juice, Clorox drops, and who-knows-what-else, but I hugged them to my chest anyway.

I dashed inside and immediately threw the pillows into the washer with lots of soap. Then I put them in the dryer with lots of Bounce sheets. The dryer had to run through several cycles. Duck feathers or goose feathers or whatever kind of feathers were in those pillows took forever to dry . . . about six hours, actually. But finally I slipped them into pillowcases and returned them to our bed.

All this activity was done on the sly, mind you, after Bill had gone to work. I certainly wasn't about to admit to Bill that he was right. That next night he didn't turn on the bedroom light, just climbed into bed and fell asleep, never realizing he was sleeping on his old, fluffy pillow once again.

The next morning, as he made the bed (one of his ways to show love), I waited for him to notice. When he was all finished, he straightened up and said, "Well, you know, I guess those new pillows are okay. You just have to get used to them."

Our circumstances aren't always so silly, but the principle still applies: If we can, with our limited visibility, see the humor in a situation, even if it's tucked off in a corner, we will find our path is an easier one.

The idea of limited vision also makes me think about where we find light. We often forget, as we struggle with our own limited visibility, that we are called to be the light of the world. Without Christian influence, the world would be a dark place. But the light that comes from our lives should serve as a beacon, attracting the lost to their Creator. Jesus said, "You are the light of the world.... Let your light so shine before men, that they may see your good works and give glory to your Father who is in heaven" (Matt. 5:14, 16 RSV). I remind myself often: "I don't have to light all the world, but I do have to light my part."

While most lighthouses have gone dark, the Boston Lighthouse, the first one in North America, shines. On Brewster Island in Boston Harbor, it beams its rays so brightly they can be seen from twenty-seven miles out at sea. Can the light you cast be seen more than twenty-seven *inches* away? Remember, the darker your environment, the brighter your light needs to be.

Different kinds of light can pierce the darkness, making the way ahead more visible: a car's headlights, the crack of lightning in an otherwise dark sky, moonlight. Perhaps the most wonderful of all is a flashlight held in the hand of someone who is searching for the one lost.

When we stumble because darkness, fog, or winding curves in the road limit our visibility, I take comfort in the thought that God knows the way ahead—he's familiar with the path I've taken to get this far. His light can and will shine even on the darkest part of the path.

When my inability to see forced me into bifocals, I complained to my ophthalmologist that I hated to have come to *this*. He patiently told me how difficult life would be if bifocals were never invented. Until bifocals, we had to make a choice; glasses could correct our vision so that we could see either far away or up close. But bifocals can do both. I would say bifocals might come in handy in our attitude toward life. It is not only our responsibility to see clearly the job at hand and do it hard and well, but we are also to have long-distance vision so we can share in God's perspective.

My ophthalmologist's explanation changed my attitude, and I stopped complaining. I became thankful for how the bifocals enhanced my vision.

This reminds me of another story.

"Wouldn't you hate to wear glasses?" one small boy asked another.

"No," said the other, "not if I could have the kind my grandma wears. My mother says she can always see when folks are tired or discouraged or sad. She sees when somebody is in need, and she can always recognize when you have something on your mind that you need to talk over. But best of all she can always see something good in everybody."

Those are called the glasses of grace, and we all need them.

A year ago Bill had a lens implant for a cataract. He seemed to be doing well until a few months later when he mentioned that seeing through that eye was like looking at objects through a piece of gauze. I hustled him right back to his ophthalmologist. I couldn't imagine what was wrong since the surgery had originally succeeded in clearing his poor vision.

The doctor explained that in many cases the clear lens can fog up with debris (after all, it is a foreign object in the eye) and chemicals can form a veil, clouding normal vision. To correct this, Bill had to have a "yag" treatment—a laser beam is carefully set to hit the lens and pierce the debris.

Sure enough, one zap with the laser beam, and the gauze effect was obliterated. Whammo! His vision was cleared.

Many things can cloud our spiritual vision: sin in our lives, separation from Christian fellowship, falling into one of the enemy's many traps. These hindrances blind us from seeing God's plans and purposes for us.

Fog is another element that blocks our visibility and makes the way hard to travel. Sometimes we find ourselves "in a fog" when we try to understand the Bible. We may strain to make it applicable to us, but we can't see the truths in the passage. At such times, we need to pray as the psalmist did, "Open my eyes that I may see wonderful things in your law" (Ps. 119:18 NIV). As we seek God's help each day, he will clear away the fog so that the marvelous truths hidden within his Word will shine through. Without the light of God's Spirit to illuminate truth, we will remain in the dark about God's Word.

It was once observed that "God has hidden every precious thing in such a way that it is a reward to the diligent, a prize to the earnest, and a joy to the finder. The nut is hidden in its thorny case; the pearl is buried beneath the ocean waves; the gold is imprisoned in the rocky bosom of the mountains; the gem is found only after you crush the rock which encloses it; the very soil gives its harvest as a reward to the laboring farmer. So truth and God must be earnestly sought."

Remember, a small trouble is like a pebble. Hold it too close to your eye, and it puts everything out of focus. Hold it at proper viewing distance, and it can be examined and classified. Throw it at your feet, and see it in its true setting—just one more tiny bump on the pathway.

Sorrow looks back, worry looks around, but faith looks up. Want to look up with me?

I once read a prayer that can help us to do just that:

"Lord, with no sense of direction I'm forever losing my way. Please tie a string from your heart to mine so that even in the darkness I'll feel the tug of your heart and find my way home."

Even with limited visibility, a prayer like that should bring us safely home.

Eight

Scenic Route

Luci Swindoll

SEAGOON: I want you to accompany me on the safari.
BLOODNOCK: Gad, sir, I'm sorry, I've never played one.
—SPIKE MILLIGAN, *THE GOON SHOW*

I should have been an explorer instead of a beauty queen. All my life I've loved poking around in backwoods, down less-traveled roads, through towns with populations of 70 to 150 people. I like stories of discovery, adventure, risk, and wandering. I even enjoy small planes that deposit me in faraway places with strange-sounding names. Something about exploring pleases my soul and keeps me in a spirit of awe and wonder. "What's around that corner?" "What's stored in that old brown shed over there?" "There's a whole field of wildflowers. Let's go picnic in them!"

To be honest, though, I'm not a very curious person—at least not about somebody's personal life. I don't care about people's financial status or who's dating whom. It would never occur to me to ask,

"How on earth did they get the money to do that?" because, even if they stole it, it's none of my business.

I'm somewhat indifferent to other folks' political views or styles of living. I figure that's between them and God, and it doesn't bother me if we differ. In fact, I'm often glad when we do because it makes for more interesting conversation and repartee.

But "Where did you go on vacation?"—now, there's a question worth spending time on. "Did you go someplace you've not been before?" "Did you and your family camp out?" "Did you travel to Europe?" "How long were you there?" "Were the people sweet to you and interesting to visit with?" "Did you enjoy the countryside or museums?" "Did you eat in cute little restaurants along the way?" "What was your favorite moment?" "Would you recommend it to others, and would you do it again?" Now we're talkin'!

Give me a good travel book by Eric Newby, Paul Theroux, Freya Stark, Peter Mayle, or a tale of intrigue and reckless adventure by Isak Dinesen or Mark Twain, and I'm a captive audience. I want all the details.

And get this: I have spent entire evenings looking at somebody's vacation slides or snapshots. "Took pictures, did you? Well, drag those babies out. I want to see them all and hear the story behind each one."

I've kept travel journals for the past thirty years of every trip I've made, and I can't count how many times I've reread them. Every word takes me back to that adventure, that year, that day, that moment in time. If it's too late to become an explorer, maybe I could be a vagabond or a cowboy. A wanderer. A nomad. Astronaut? *Calm down, Lucille . . . just stay with the job at hand.*

Charles Kuralt (one of my favorite radio and television news correspondents as well as travel authors) said, "The good memories are all of stopping and staying awhile. I realize I've always driven too fast through life, carrying in my baggage too much impatience and apprehension, missing too many chances, passing too many good people in the dust."[1]

When we consider our journey through life and the short time we're here, it's important that we take the back roads sometimes, that we stop and stay awhile. This may be difficult in today's fast-paced world, but if we don't take the byways as well as the freeways, we will miss one of life's most enjoyable benefits—the scenic route.

This past summer, my wonderful friend and frequent traveling companion, Mary, and I went to Africa. She had been before, about eight years ago, and I had wanted to go since I was a teenager. We'd planned this trip for two years. We read everything we could get our hands on about Africa in general and Kenya in particular. We watched videos of safaris. We studied pictures of wild animals, learning their names and habitats. On more than one occasion, we pulled out maps and an atlas or two comparing distances between point A and point B. We bought books about what to take, where to stay, when to go. Friends who had been there and those who presently live there suggested modes of travel and how to make the most of our nine days. We watched *Out of Africa* and *The Lion King* over and over. We saved our money. I mean, we were *serious* about this venture, and it was a huge investment of time, energy, and money.

We agreed on several non-negotiables: We would *not* go with a tour group; we would stay in a tented camp by a river; we would travel with as few clothes and as much camera equipment as possible; and we would pray that every animal we had read about would cross our path during our sojourn.

Eventually our itinerary was set: three days in a tent in the Maasai Mara; one day in Nairobi (so we could actually take a bath and do laundry); four days in the Aberdere National Park; and one night at The Ark, famous for nighttime viewing of the animals

---

[1]Charles Kuralt, *A Life on the Road* (Norwalk, Conn.: The Easton Press, 1990), 245.

who come to sip from a pool of water or lick from the giant salt deposit in the ground. Talk about a scenic route!

Upon leaving the States we claimed Proverbs 16:3: "Commit to the LORD whatever you do, and your plans will succeed" (NIV). Every night away, we prayed, putting our hope in the Lord for his protection and provision. And he brought both . . . in abundance.

We had the adventure of a lifetime. On the second morning, as we slept soundly in our zipped up tent, our alarm went off at 5 A.M. We didn't mind; we were too excited. This was the day we would ride in a hot-air balloon over the northern part of the Serengeti Plain.

Mary and I had requested that one of the attendants at Governor's Camp bring us coffee, and not ten minutes after the alarm sounded, he appeared with a tray of steaming hot Kenyan coffee and little biscuits to help us greet the day. "*Jambo mama*," he said from the front porch, which means "hello, mama." He then proceeded to unzip the tent and walk right into our room, which was heretofore shrouded in darkness. He carried, in addition to the tray, a huge Coleman lantern that illuminated the entire area. Fortunately, I had slipped into the bathroom (in another zippered area), but Mary lay in bed as this total stranger set the tray on the night table right beside her, lit a candle, took a few steps backward, then turned and disappeared out the zippered doorway. I heard him leave and I stuck my head out of the bathroom.

We looked at each other and yelled in our loudest, predawn whisper, "We're on safari!" I think we realized right then that the days ahead would be unlike any we had ever experienced. New faces. Wild animals. Different languages. Zippered rooms. Dancing tribesmen. Everything about this trip would be an adventure, and we were hyped.

Fortified by the hot coffee and the sheer anticipation of what lay ahead, we left the tent just as a slight glow from the still-sleeping sun broke on the distant horizon. We were escorted to the waiting Land Rover and taken to the Mara River, where we crossed by boat to the adjacent bank. By this time we heard voices, people in the distance chatting and laughing. As we approached a huge flat, grassy area, we saw the two largest hot-air balloons in the world being inflated; soon, twenty-four of us would drift silently above the Mara for our photographic safari.

Pilots and passengers alike busily prepared to take off in these monstrous modes of transport. Flames from the balloon burners began to light up the area, and the first pink tongues of sunlight flickered in the clouds above.

A short time later, Mary and I reveled in the beauty as we floated over plains, forests, and little tributaries of the Mara River, snapping pictures like two fledgling *National Geographic* scouts. I was surprised that we could so clearly hear the sounds below: a lion's roar, elephants crashing through the bush, warthogs stomping in and out of their holes, and herds of impala and giraffe running for cover, startled by this colorful, silent, giant ball hovering over them.

After our landing on a group of termite mounds, we crawled out of the basket and shared a delicious champagne breakfast, cooked to perfection on the balloon's burners, right there on the savanna under the all-staring eyes of great herds of zebra and wildebeests.

"Don't wake me when this is over," I warned Mary.

I may never recover from those nine days of African safari, and I'm not sure I want to. It's okay by me if it stays imprinted on my mind and heart forever. I learned several things on that scenic route in the rich, vast, gorgeous country of Kenya that I will use as a measure for all side roads and vacations from now on.

I think the greatest benefit of getting away from the known course, and taking the less-traveled road, is to experience the unspoiled beauty of nature and the wonder of God's creation. For example, our Land Rover might start out on an existing road, but then without the slightest provocation, our driver would leave that well-defined way and make a road of his own. Untrodden. Unmarked. Unexpected and unknown before we turned. A brand-new path out into the national reserve someplace. Mary and I would look at each other, muttering, "How did he know to turn here?"

But as we would proceed down this unfettered pathway, we would come upon the most amazing beauty. Never mind that we ran over tall grass, tree stumps, animal dung, and ruts sometimes six inches deep and full of water. Never mind that we drove under low-thorny limbs, vulture-laden branches, and monkeys swinging from tree to tree. We were on a mission—to see wild animals.

And did we see them? Numerous times: five cheetahs resting under the only shade tree in an expanse the size of New Jersey; a male lion with seventeen cubs, eating the rib cage of a zebra; the kill of a leopard hanging in an obscure tree, while the baby leopard slept atop the adjoining tree; huge rhinos shaped like mini-buses galloping after us, as only a fat rhino can; herds of elephants crossing the Mara River, bathing themselves and each other; giraffes enjoying breakfast, as they craned their necks to retrieve some delicate morsel atop the highest branch of an acacia tree.

Almost without exception, the very best viewing of these beautiful creatures was way off the road. We never knew how our driver found his way there, and more importantly, how he got us back to camp.

At times, on life's journey, taking the scenic route is exactly what is needed to rejuvenate our harried, frazzled spirits. We've driven the freeway and taken the predictable path long enough. We're tired. We need to leave our impatience and apprehension behind us and try something new. Refreshment comes when we do this.

It's true that the journey can often become less than joyful. We've had it! We've had it with the kids, we've had it with our job, we've had it with our loved ones, we've had it with life. All the joy is gone.

When you reach this state of mind, you need to change your scenery. Take a break. I don't mean you have to run away from home (although you might consider that), nor do you have to board a plane bound for a foreign land. You don't even have to get in your car.

Next time you're in the grocery store, buy a package of flower seeds and plant them in a little bed in your backyard just for your soul. Water it and tend it every day. Or what about that ugly room, the one at the end of the hall you've always wished would fall in during the next earthquake? Paint it or hang new drapes. As Timon in *The Lion King* says, "Talk about your fixer upper." Snazz it up. Make it sparkle. Give it zest. You do not have to walk down that hallway and look at the same old drab room forever and ever. *You* can change it.

If you live alone and are sick of your mundane life, make a few alterations. Find a new way to greet the day. Take a different route to work, even if it takes longer. Leave earlier and play your favorite music all the way to the office—sing along at the top of your lungs. Plan a trip with a good friend and start saving a little money each month. It can be done. The point is, don't let the beaten path you travel daily beat you down. If you want to see new sights, hear different sounds, speak refreshing words, leave your baggage of fear, regret, guilt, and disappointment behind you and say, "I'm outta here. I'm going to try another way of getting to joy." This new venture may seem scary or strange to you, but don't let that stop you.

This poem by Robert Frost depicts a man off the beaten path:

Whose woods these are I think I know,
His house is in the village though;
He will not see me stopping here
To watch his woods fill up with snow,
My little horse must think it queer
To stop without a farmhouse near

Between the woods and frozen lake
The darkest evening of the year.
He gives his harness bells a shake
To ask if there is some mistake.
The only other sound's the sweep
Of easy wind and downy flake.
The woods are lovely, dark and deep,
But I have promises to keep,
And miles to go before I sleep,
And miles to go before I sleep.[2]

This lovely poem describes the beauty a certain driver will miss if he fails to take time for the scenic route. He pulls off the known path and into the woods to watch the trees and ground fill up with snow. He doesn't plan to stay long; nor is it necessary. He only wants to take a moment to refresh his soul.

The horse is eager to leave, shaking his harness bells as if inquiring after the lone man's sanity in stopping in the first place. The driver has always rushed, and he has forced his little horse to do the same. *Why are we doing this?* the horse might be thinking. Then, as though he has captured the moment in his mind, he mentally shakes himself and hastens away.

The scenic route need not take a long time nor be far from home, but it must be something that will refresh our souls, lift us from our dailyness, and cause us to see the wonder of God in a new, different way.

Sometimes a fascinating part of the scenic path is the people we meet along the way—if indeed, there are any. Oftentimes, an off-the-road experience involves no one but ourselves.

In Africa Mary and I noticed a joy in the Kenyan nationals that was contagious. They didn't seem burdened by the commer-

[2]Robert Frost, *Complete Poems of Robert Frost* (New York: Holt, Rinehart and Winston, 1964), 275.

cialism that often plagues North America. So what if fifty people ended up on a bus designed to hold only twenty? "There's always room for one more," they would say with a smile. "*Hakuna matata*" . . . no worries. Little seemed to bother them; they had so little in the first place and had learned to be happy with what they had. Children on the side of the road would wave and smile at every passing vehicle.

Near the end of our safari, we stayed in a room with a fireplace, and each night an attendant would come, turn down our beds, and build a huge, roaring fire that would last all night. He accomplished this with only three pieces of kindling, two sheets of newspaper, and one match. One evening Mary and I watched in awe as he got the fire blazing once again with so little effort.

"How is it you never need more than one match?" Mary asked him. "I've used up practically an entire box of matches building a fire in my fireplace."

He grinned broadly and told us how he built a fire every night in his own home. His mother cooked over the fire, as well as heated water for bathing. The fire kept them warm when it was cold. He reported all of this with great delight; he was proud of the way his family lived. "It is very nice," he said. "I like to make the fire, and we all enjoy it in our house."

What we might see as an inconvenience, he viewed as a pleasure. I realize he probably has no basis of comparison, and I don't want to romanticize his lifestyle, but nevertheless comparison is often our greatest problem. We compare constantly. We look at what others have and we want it—all of it. We think it will make us happier. When we acquire such and such, we'll be content and quit worrying. Would that we could say "*Hakuna matata*" now, before we have to buy or own one more thing.

In the course of my travels, I have come to know many interesting people—those who speak other languages and those who speak no English whatsoever. Those who hold to very different political and spiritual views than I. Those who are highly educated and those who never went to school. I have visited in their homes, used sign language to make myself understood, shared meals and opinions with them, and become a close friend to many of them.

One of my dearest friends is of Greek nationality. Sophia Stylianidou lives in Athens. We have corresponded for twenty-eight years, and I have been to visit her and her family on eight different occasions. We happened to meet because I walked off the beaten path and wandered into the shop where she worked. I was traveling with two other friends, and we invited Sophia to join us for dinner. She accepted, and we have kept in touch ever since, even though we live more than six thousand miles apart.

Knowing this wonderful person through life's joys and sorrows has enhanced me immeasurably. I am a better person because of her influence, and I trust she feels the same. Although Sophia and I differ in many ways, we love each other as though we were sisters. I thank God for putting her in my pathway so many years ago.

I have been traveling since 1966, the year of my first passport. I have spent time in thirteen different countries and traveled all over the United States. I absolutely love to travel. Give me a map, point me in a direction, and I'm on my way.

My work with the other three Joyful Journey speakers calls for a great deal of travel. I never tire of it. Sometimes I wish I had more space between trips to pack or unpack, but generally speaking, even that doesn't bother me.

Still, despite all of the scenic routes stored in my travel diaries and in my heart, I am aware it's very possible to desire a change in our lives and spend years where it looks like nothing at all is happening. Lots of people live that way day after day. I believe that to simply desire change is not enough. Action must accompany desire if we want to set the change in motion. And it all starts with prayer. God has all sorts of unbelievable, wonderful, exciting adventures out there on the horizon of our lives. He is capable of changing anything.

Mary and I wanted to see every animal possible while we were in Africa. When would we ever be back? So we made plans to see all we could, from the "big five"—elephant, rhino, leopard, cape buffalo, and lion—right down to the little Rock Hyrax that resembles a guinea pig. We prayed to that end and hoped it would come to pass.

Friends who had lived in Kenya for ten, twelve, even eighteen years told us they had never seen a leopard, the most elusive of the cat family. We should not be disappointed, we were told, if we didn't see one. Well, we not only saw one—we saw four! We saw the mother and baby (with the kill hanging in the tree), and on the last day of the final game drive, we saw two more within ten minutes of one another. They were so close we could have reached out and petted them. 'Course, it would have been the last animal we ever petted . . . but they actually stopped, posed for my camera, and waited for me to shoot, reload, and shoot again. Beautiful creatures. Anyway, we saw every one of the big five and every other animal that inhabits that area, I do believe. Mary and I planned our course, doing everything we possibly could to fulfill our wish, but God gave us the fulfillment.

In Proverbs 16:9 we read, "In his heart a man plans his course, but the LORD determines his steps" (NIV). Only God had the ability to bring the leopard, the rarest of animals on the African continent, into our view. And during the daylight? Unheard of. "You are lucky to have seen a miracle," our driver told us after seeing the leopards. But we believed it was an answer to prayer. We desired it. We prayed about it. We planned for it. And God brought it to pass.

On your own journey, can you dare to ask God for something really different? Unusual? Wonderful? Unique? I can't promise you he will do it, but I do know that when we leave our choices with him, he frequently takes us off the beaten thoroughfare and into the woods to watch the snow fall, or through a shop door to meet a new friend, or down a rough path toward a treasure at the end, or even into his waiting arms that will ultimately give us peace.

I often read books about traveling. Recently, I found this marvelous promise that each of us can embrace: "Sit down anywhere you like, on a wall, a stone, a tree stump, on the grass or the earth: everywhere they surround you, a painting and a poem, everywhere the world resonates beautifully and happily around you."[3]

---

[3]Hermann Hesse, *Wandering* (New York: Farrar, Straus & Giroux, 1972), 49.

Nine

Watch for Falling Rocks

Patsy Clairmont

Follow the yellow brick road.
—E. Y. Harburg, *The Wizard of Oz*

Michigan in autumn is absolutely intoxicating. Wine-colored leaves swagger midair in one last hurrah and then swirl to the ground. They join a profusion of amber, orange, and red leaves forming a quilted kaleidoscope. With winter so near, how kind of autumn to wrap the earth in warm hues.

I talked to my niece Cheryl last night. She sounded so weary. Life had been a swirl of activities, and she was left reeling. I longed to wrap her in a colorful quilt, serve her hot cocoa, and read her a story. Of course, Cheryl's husband and three teenage sons might have thought that odd. But there are times in a woman's life when she could use a little coddling. Ask me.

Actually I'd like to see a national "Coddle a Woman" holiday established. On this joyous day we would but speak our fondest desire, and it would be ours: a three-hour bath in rose petals, a two-hour pedicure, a peppermint foot massage, a delicious nap, a maid with manners, macadamias dripping in chocolate, an endless symphony, and our dearest friend's undivided attention. How's that for starters?

Unfortunately, life seldom offers us this kind of decadent indulgence. Instead, it is rather brisk and risky. Harsh winds and falling rocks are often the order of the day. Swirls of bills, reeling relationships, and staggering demands. Not to mention people who fling rocky retorts, cast stony glares, and throw out hard bottom lines. We dash down life's congested highways at breakneck speeds only to encounter (watch out!) falling debris. Rocks litter our journey and attempt to crush our joy.

Take note of the word *attempt*. Archaic individuals (like Luci, Marilyn, Barbara, and me) define *attempt* as: "to attack with the intention of subduing" and "to tempt." A clear example of attacking with the intention of subduing would be Marilyn when her dessert arrives at the table. This woman is proficient at subduing a dessert. And tempt is what she does to me. You see, Marilyn has such finely attuned culinary taste buds I can hardly help myself. I see her tasty dessert, and the next thing I know, I have my fork in it. I know, I know, we've been down this rocky road before. (I love that flavor.)

The enemy, the true (at)tempter, is ecstatic when he can stir up a landslide to throw us off course. We are talking really rocky. He would like to create such a raucous diversion that we would be intimidated, defeated, and overwhelmed. But here is the kicker: *Attempt* also means "to try." This suggests the Old Stone Thrower isn't always successful when he slings his projectiles in our direction. We can duck, dodge, and yes, even defy his attempts. But to be successful we need God's help and the right equipment.

I love equipment, especially professional equipment. I like to look as if I know what I'm doing. When I took up cross-country skiing, I was a sight to behold. Not only as I slipped and slid toward my first little hill but also as they swept up my parts at the bottom of the hill. The equipment suffered, as did I; a layer of rocks lay under the deceptive layer of fluffy snow. My downfall was to think good equipment made a skier. I had forgotten a few essentials such as lessons and experience. So it is with God. Having his Word without studying it and practicing it won't save us from the Hefty Hurler.

Nowadays, it seems all equipment requires a doctoral degree and another two years of practical working experience if a person is to make any use of it at all. And there's nothing practical about equipment. For instance, take my computer. Please, take my computer. I look professional seated behind it, but one of us has rocks in our system. My dad used to tell me I had rocks in my head, so it could be me that's causing the hardship between us. I am improving, though. I can now turn on the computer, type text, and exit. And recently I even entered the world of online.

Talk about rock throwing. Whoa! Big-time rock hurling events can occur in that arena. I enjoy visiting in the chat booths with folks from all over the country. I've met some dynamic people, but I've encountered cyberspace rockettes as well. They heave themselves through the Internet pitching insults and oaths at unsuspecting visitors. Their disruptive approach seems to give the violators a sick sense of importance. The hurlers attempt to subdue the chat booth by becoming a negative center of attention and tempting the chatters into vicious verbal volleys. Sometimes they're successful; sometimes they're not. Gratefully, cyberspace cops search out these online outlaws and toss them onto the proverbial rock pile. (That's when they lose their online privileges for a time.)

Les did an extravagant thing several years ago and gave me a sparkling bracelet of "rocks." It was gorgeous. The bracelet came with a double lock to insure its safety, which I was grateful for since I travel so much.

Three months after receiving it I flew to Oklahoma to speak for a ladies event and then returned home. I walked into our bedroom, sat down on the edge of the bed, and began to tell Les about my trip. Suddenly I realized my bracelet was gone. A panicky feeling rose up in me as I searched through my coat lining and then retraced my steps to the car. After carefully sorting through my luggage, I called the hotel where I had stayed and offered a reward. I also contacted the airport and reported it missing. But after I explained my dilemma, the woman at the airport said, "Now let me get this straight. You lost a bracelet full of diamonds, and you think someone will turn it in?" My heart sank. The following day Les called our insurance company to report the loss only to learn that our policy did not cover jewelry. To make matters worse, it wasn't even paid for . . . groan.

After losing my lovely gift from Les, I seemed to give myself a self-inflicted prison sentence. I hammered away at myself for my negligence. I refused Les's offer to replace my diamond bracelet and made him promise to never again buy me fancy baubles. Whenever I noticed someone else wearing a lovely piece of jewelry, I felt the sting of both loss and guilt. Whenever I dressed up, I would long for the bracelet to adorn my wrist.

A year went by, and I was still angry with myself. I had allowed the loss of my bracelet to put a major dent in my joy.

I finally had a breakthrough one day when I realized lost rocks were not worth stoning myself over. So, I learned one method for dodging the Stone Thrower's projectiles: let go of guilt and forgive myself.

Les and I knew my prison sentence had ended and that I was truly over the loss and my failure when one Christmas I suggested a bracelet would make a thoughtful gift for me. I now have recovered so well that Les has suggested I take up rock climbing.

Do you need to defy the Stone Thrower by forgiving yourself? Perhaps you have lost something—or someone. Feeling unforgiven is like swallowing a rock; everywhere you go you feel the weight and discomfort of your failure. This sets you up for depression and a spreading inner hardness. You may feel the need to punish yourself, which only adds internal pressure, leaving you volcanic. You then might begin to spew words like fiery rocks singeing those who pass by.

I recently overheard a woman on my flight tell her seatmate she had been living in another country in which it was still an accepted practice to stone people for certain crimes. But now, instead of a crowd hurling stones as in Bible times, a dump truck would back up and release a whole load of falling rocks onto the convicted person.

What a crushing blow—literally. This form of punishment gives new dynamics to the old "sticks and stones may break my bones" rhyme. I'm so grateful for Jesus' compassionate response to the woman the crowd was about to stone for her adulterous behavior. Imagine an angry mob of people with raised rocks and haughty hearts positioned to pummel you with their judgment. Then Jesus steps into their midst, and with piercing conviction, turns to you, extends undeserved mercy, and proclaims, "Go your way; . . . sin no more" (John 8:11 NASB).

I don't have proof, but I would imagine that the adulterous woman never returned to her former behavior. Not because she feared dying, for she probably wished many times that she could escape her sinful passions and her guilt-ridden self-esteem. But because Jesus had liberated her with his forgiveness. It was her chance for a new beginning, a fresh start, a clean slate.

I am in a "new beginning" time of my life as Les and I have just moved into a new home. As we prepared to move, we dug into the recesses of our basement, closets, and attic (cough, cough). We shook out long-forgotten rugs, old coverlets, and dusty lamp shades (achoo). We've pruned some of our contents so that we can fit into our awaiting home (hooray). When moving day arrived, we were enthused about our chance to begin anew with clean cupboards, tidy drawers, and spic-and-span corners.

In the same way, the Lord enters into the interior of our being and begins to set us in order. When Jesus penetrates our rocky hearts a transformation occurs. "Old things [have] passed away; behold, new things have come" (2 Cor. 5:17 NASB). He will even assist us in removing any fallen rocks that may be crushing our spirit. And it is not easy to find rock movers. Throwers are plentiful, movers are sparse. (I discovered this when I decided to build a rock wall in my garden.)

What causes a heart to harden? Being pelted with pride, resentment, loss, unfairness, rejection, misunderstanding, disappointment, and abuse. In other words—life. Sometimes it feels as if life has backed up and unloaded a truck full of rocks on us.

But here is the good news—those rocks are gems in disguise. We may need some spiritual Murine in order to see the sparkle beneath the crusty surface, but life can't throw any rocks our way that the Lord can't transform. So we don't have to feel constantly intimidated or overwhelmed. Yes, at times we will feel bombarded by falling rocks, but we have a Comforter—One who knows every hair on our heads and every bruise in our hearts.

It's true that, on occasion, others will throw rocks in our direction; we become the recipient of their hostile behavior. Also, we can allow our hearts to form a rocky resistance to life, causing us to become receptacles of our own hostility. *Or* we can receive the Savior and be reconciled to God, which will turn our hostilities into hosannas. Ezekiel says it this way: "Moreover, I will give you a new heart and put a new spirit within you; and I will remove the heart of stone from your flesh and give you a heart of flesh" (Ezek. 36:26 NASB).

When I was eight years old, a girl from my neighborhood threw an insult at me, and I popped her square on the nose with my fist. I was horrified as blood began to pour from her nostrils. While it was a minor injury, it made a major impact on me. I never again popped anyone with my fist. Instead, my rock-throwing hostility took the form of verbal stoning and personal indicting.

Then I met Jesus and learned that he didn't want me to throw rocks, allow myself to be buried under them, or let them form in my heart. Instead, he wanted me to stand on the foundational rock of Christ. The sweet psalmist David said, "He brought me up out of the pit of destruction, out of the miry clay; and He set my feet upon a rock making my footsteps firm" (Ps. 40:2 NASB).

As a boy, my friend Randy drove frequently with his family through the mountains, and they would often come upon a Watch for Falling Rocks sign. His mother told him that Falling Rocks was the name of a young Indian boy who was lost. The signs reminded motorists to watch for him. Randy remembers driving through the craggy country, ever vigilantly watching for signs of little Falling Rocks.

Well, our Rock isn't lost; *au contraire*, Jesus is seeking the lost. He has promised to come again and receive us unto himself. (Hosanna!) He is not returning to coddle us but to collect us up for his higher purposes. (Hosanna!) The Lord promised to leave signs so that we might know when the time of his appearing was near. (Hosanna!) May we be vigilant sisters, for our Rock and Redeemer draweth nigh. (Come, Lord Jesus.)

 Ten

Slower Traffic Keep Right

Marilyn Meberg

I journeyed fur, I journeyed fas'; I glad I foun' de place at las'!

—JOEL CHANDLER HARRIS, *NIGHTS WITH UNCLE REMUS*

Even if I have no particular destination, I have to get there fast! No way in the world will anyone catch me in the "right lane" on this life journey—unless, of course, I need to chat with Luci.

I've never really understood my driving passion for life's fast pace. Although I'm capable of quiet contemplation, hours of immersion in a great book, or soul chats in front of the fireplace, I feel an irresistible pull to anything that promises the sensation of speed.

In fact, my penchant for driving fast produced so many speeding tickets one year that were I to receive one more, I would have lost my license. My long-suffering husband, in an effort to impose driving temperance and to avoid tickets as well as the yearly traffic school experience, suggested we buy a diesel-run car. I was unenthusiastic but could certainly see the wisdom in this idea. So we purchased a sturdy German vehicle that imbibed and belched only diesel.

You probably know that it's impossible to jack-rabbit from a stoplight with a diesel engine. The diesel motor takes all movement under advisement and then, after due consideration, rolls forward, but generally not without spewing a bit of black resistance through the tailpipe. Handicapped though I was to make my mark on the highway, I found myself oddly charmed by the deepthroated guttural engine tones that enveloped me as I drove. These tones, as well as the resolute car body, suggested a sense of security and a stalwart dependability that made me feel safe. I named the car Gretchen and grew to love her unwavering spirit. And not only did I develop a warm relationship with her, but my driving record also improved enormously. I did manage, however, to acquire one speeding ticket in the ten years I drove this car, but for the most part, Ken's goals were accomplished. I, of necessity, slowed down, and even discovered some merits in driving at a more sedate pace. I can't recall them now, of course, having returned to my original love of speed.

Although Ken, in all his fifty-two years of living, never received a speeding ticket, he was nonetheless a fun-loving and adventure-endorsing guy. He simply did not share my passion for the fast lane. However, once in our thirty years together I thought I might actually have won him over to my speed zone.

We were celebrating my fortieth birthday at my favorite Italian restaurant. (I truly believe the food of heaven will be Italian; just the scent of garlic sautéing in butter puts me at heaven's door, not to mention the image of al dente noodles slathered in Alfredo sauce and sporting a generous topping of Romano cheese . . . Mercy, we've gone through the portals!) We began to discuss our ages and specific recreational activities we had not yet accomplished but wanted to before age interfered. As we enumerated our respective "must do" desires, Ken's orderly mind prompted him to whip out pen and paper and make a Marilyn list and a Ken list. Then we prioritized our lists. At the top of his list was white-water rafting, and at the top of mine was skiing. Neither of us had done either.

Quite frankly, I had no interest in white-water rafting. I feared the motion would produce a socially unacceptable physiological response, and I also didn't relish sleeping on the ground in spite of the kind of tent that promises protection from bugs. The whole experience sounded like a punishment reserved for those guilty of serious misconduct.

By the same token, Ken had no interest in skiing. Now, it seemed perfectly clear to me why white-water rafting would be unappealing, but how on earth could anyone not want to ski? "Just imagine," I coaxed Ken, "how exhilarating it would feel to swoop down a snowy mountain leaving a plume of snow in your wake. And can't you just see yourself gracefully swishing left and then right down a steep slope at a speed that nearly seals your eyes shut but over which you have complete control and from which you won't even get a ticket?"

For a brief moment his eyes shined at these images, and I victoriously said to myself, *The seed is taking root. I knew he would like that part about being in control!*

However, three birthdays passed, and we had neither skied nor rafted. Ken took far better care of others than he did of himself, and it was always a challenge to persuade him to take time off from work. Then Ken's best friend, Orvie Hampton, informed a group of our dear friends that we were all going skiing together the last week in January. He had rented a big condo in Mammoth and told Ken to put the dates on his calendar. I was thrilled out of my mind.

Then, a week before we were due to leave for Mammoth, Ken began to murmur things like:

"I really shouldn't leave the office this time of the year."

"I'm going to miss a crucial board meeting."

"Why do we need to go? I don't even want to ski. Did you put Orvie up to this?"

The day before we were supposed to leave, Ken called me from his office complaining of a sore throat and the beginnings of a runny nose. I, of course, commiserated but didn't suggest that he should stay home.

You see, I knew Ken's pattern. Whenever he felt coerced into something he didn't want to do, he managed to catch a cold that frequently would get him off the hook.

During the six-hour drive to Mammoth, Ken hunched behind the steering wheel sneezing, snorting, and blowing. I chatted cheerfully the whole trip and held the tissue box for his convenience. Ken's spirits did pick up later as we sat around the huge, log-burning fireplace in the spectacular condo Orvie had rented. We laughed, ate, and told the kinds of stories only those people can who have known and cared for each other for years.

Lying in bed beside Ken that night, I was aware of his restlessness and periodic sniffing and sneezing. When he realized I was awake he said, "Marilyn, you know how we talked about taking a ski lesson before we go out on the slopes in the morning?"

"Yes."

"Well, I don't want to take a group lesson. Let's just get a lesson for the two of us. Is that okay?"

"Absolutely. I would feel better about that."

"Good. That's what we'll do."

Soon he was asleep. It was then that possible reasons for Ken's resistance to skiing began to come into focus for me. For one thing, he was a bit overweight; maybe he was worried about his ability to swoop gracefully down the slopes. Also, he might have worried that, because I am quite athletic, I would pick up the skills more quickly than he, and he wouldn't look good. I was filled with compassion. I would preserve his ego at all costs. Such a sweet, dear man. I would be tender with him.

The next morning, as I sipped my last cup of tea and watched the skiers making their way down the snow-packed road toward the ski lift, I could hardly contain myself. Finally I was going to ski! I would feel the wind-whipped snow flying past my face as the nearly airborne thrust took me flying down the picture-perfect slopes!

Orvie taught us how to put on our ski boots and suggested we do so before taking the stairs down to the street. As I squeezed my feet into the boots, I felt as if I were strapped into that kind of concrete molding used for the construction of bridges. These boots had absolutely no give, no bend whatsoever for the ankles.

As we clunked woodenly down the stairs and onto the street, Ken told our friends to go on and we would catch up later. With my skis tossed casually over my shoulder (that's how I saw other skiers carrying them), I periodically handed Ken tissues and wondered if his boots were as unyielding as mine. He wasn't complaining. I thought maybe I had the wrong size.

When we arrived at Warming Hut Two (an odd name for what I assumed was a ski lodge), Ken said he would go in and make arrangements for our lessons. I asked him to first please help me put on my skis. I thought maybe the boots would feel more comfortable attached to the skis. With difficulty, we managed to clamp me in. The clamping sounded like the ominous slam of an iron door. I felt irrevocably committed.

Ken then suggested I "stay put," and he would return with an instructor. I smiled weakly. I really didn't have a choice in the matter. I didn't feel even a hint of potential mobility. At least I didn't think so . . . until I sensed the gradual backward sliding of my skis. I looked down to see that I was standing on a slight slope that stretched down to a concrete abutment a few feet away. I seemed unable to stop the sliding.

When Ken returned with Debbie, our instructor, they found me in a pigeon-toed position, scrunched awkwardly against the wall. Ken rushed over, pulled me into place, and introduced me to Debbie.

He effortlessly clamped on his skis, and then Debbie led us to a bunny slope where she showed us how to go up the hill sideways, ski down, and snowplow to a stop. It looked too easy.

Unfortunately, the snow was slinging itself at my face with such biting ferocity that I had to pull my scarf up to my eyebrows for protection. I had found the short walk on the world's longest skis to the bunny slope quite an exertion, and my glasses were so steamy I could barely see. Ken offered to go first thus giving my glasses time to clear up.

He expertly scaled the little slope quickly and efficiently, lifting one ski crossways over the other, and then, just as efficiently, came down the slope, pointing his skis toward each other as Debbie shouted, "Now snowplow."

I yelled my congratulations to Ken, who beamed up at me. "Your turn, Marilyn," he called.

Eager to perform as well as Ken, I pushed off with a lurching motion that threw me immediately off balance. Then, when Debbie shouted, "Snowplow," I twisted my unwieldy skis so abruptly that not only did they turn in, but they also crossed over each other, cutting me off at the groin. I repeated this several times, and Debbie asked if I would like to continue practicing while she took Ken over to the puma lift since he was obviously ready for the next step. A look of satisfaction crossed Ken's face, and I realized I hadn't seen him blow his nose or even sniff in the last thirty minutes. I told them I'd go with them, get the puma instruction (whatever that was), and then backtrack to the little slope for future mastery.

By the time I managed to lurch and lunge over to the puma location, Debbie had already shown Ken how to catch the motorized rope connected to numbers of strategically spaced little wooden disks upon which one sat while being pulled up the slope. I figured I didn't really need the explanation anyway; it was clear what one needed to do.

Since my glasses had fogged up once more, Ken volunteered to go ahead. I watched him as the rope and disk swooped up behind him. He grabbed the rope, then straddled the disk, and was carried off in one fluid motion. "Piece of cake, Marilyn," he called over his shoulder.

"I wonder why his glasses don't fog up?" I muttered.

I had no time for further musings, as Debbie shouted, "Okay, Marilyn, grab the rope and straddle the disk!" I was so startled by the sudden need to grab and straddle, I missed the rope, grabbed the disk, and fell facedown into the snow while the puma disk swung on by.

Ken continued to flawlessly perform each maneuver while I continued various versions of failure. If I grabbed the rope, I dropped my poles. If I held my poles, I dropped the rope. When I grabbed the rope and held my poles, I missed the disk.

Having successfully completed the puma challenge, Ken was now ready for the chairlift instruction a good distance away. He came swishing left and right down the slope toward me, executed a perfect snowplow stop inches from me, and asked if I minded that he go on over for the chairlift instruction. I encouraged him to do so, assuring him I would join him shortly. He noticed then that I was sneezing and doing some sniffing, and so he handed me a tissue before he glided off with Debbie.

The puma experience included additional challenges beyond just taming the rope and the disk. On arriving at the top of the slope (and I did manage to succeed at that a few times), I was faced with the nerve-racking task of getting back down. This was difficult because I couldn't seem to manage the snowplow maneuver. I suspected the reason was the odd way the skis seemed to grow longer and longer with the passing of time. They had more than doubled in length in just the short time they had worn me.

However, far more troubling than the puma and the skis was my presence as the only adult on the bunny slope. Not only was I surrounded by children, most of whom found me an annoyance, but many of them were handicapped. Several had only one leg, and a number of them only one arm. I watched as these kids effortlessly mounted the puma disk and then effortlessly swooped down the slope in spite of their missing limbs; it was personally indicting.

One little guy, about ten years old and missing his left leg, decided I was sufficiently pitiful to warrant his constant coaching. I hated to appear ungracious, but I have to admit I failed to truly appreciate his efforts. He patiently explained over and over again that I needed to learn to snowplow instead of merely falling into the snowdrift when I wanted to stop. I didn't think he would understand the mysterious and persistent growth of my skis, so I didn't even bother to explain.

Finally and mercifully, my little coach called down into the depths of a particularly deep snowdrift that had claimed me. "Maybe you should go home," he suggested. As I lay there entangled in my gargantuan skis, I envisioned the fireplace in the condo, me in front of it, reading my book and relishing a cup of hot tea.

That was the best coaching he'd given me so far. And so, with the help of my little friend, I managed not only to extricate myself from the snowbank but also to get my skis off and clunk home.

Hours later, many hours later, when Ken and the others burst into the condo with ruddy cheeks and sparkling eyes, Ken rushed over to my easy chair. "I know what you mean about speed, Marilyn," he burst out, "that feeling of racing down the slope so fast your eyes are nearly sealed shut and yet knowing all the time you're in control. There's nothing like it!"

I smiled wanly. "I'm so glad for you, Babe," I mumbled.

He looked at me for a moment and asked how I was. I assured him I was fine except for a runny nose and a sore throat.

Isn't that the way life is? I get my wish and can't handle it. Ken slogs along without enthusiasm and then discovers he's having a great time. I think I want speed and end up in the snowbank. Ken thinks he wants to be anywhere but swooshing down the slope and finds it an exhilarating experience.

Life likes to throw surprises in our faces. We picture how a certain event, a longed-for expectation, will turn out. Some of our imaginings can be quite detailed—and wonderful. Then, when the real thing comes along, it is nothing like we imagined.

Sometimes we can adjust our fantasy to match the reality, but at other times, we just need to move off the slope or out of the fast lane and sit down a spell to recover. This is certainly true when it comes to marriage and motherhood. Growing up, most of us get caught in the fantasy of finding and marrying our prince, living in the castle, and filling that castle with little cherubs.

Ever notice how no one mentions how much work the prince, the castle, and the cherubs are? Next thing you know you're living in the fast lane—or at least in a van—unsure of how you got there. It's not that you don't love your prince, your castle, or your cherubs. But it all requires a lot more of you than you had counted on. And it often feels like you're driving too fast to control the vehicle. You aren't alone, sister. If you holler for help, the woman in the Jeep next to you can lend a hand. She will almost certainly admit that the emotional and physical demands on her are in overdrive. But if she's been on the road a little longer, she may know it better, and can help guide you through some of the curves and merging lanes up ahead.

Despite some of the dangers of the fast lane, I have to confess it's not just the sensation of speed that keeps me there; it's the wonderful feeling of accomplishment as I quickly finish my various tasks and duties. I love that delicious sense of being the one ahead of "the game," the leader of the pack, and other such identities with undoubtedly primitive origins.

But I'll tell you something that amazes and humbles me—and puts me in my place. Barbara Johnson leaves me in the dust! That dear woman is an absolute dynamo; no way can I keep up with her. She rises every morning around five and calls various persons around the country who have written to her in total despair over their son with AIDS or their daughter who has announced she is a lesbian. Barbara encourages these parents to trust in God's love in spite of their heartbreak. She makes herself totally available—no secretary, no unlisted phone number. I can't count how many people have told me they are alive today because of Barbara.

She does scores of guest spot radio shows every week, and she and Bill put out their monthly newsletter (mailed to more than five thousand people) themselves. No staff, no help whatsoever. I asked her a silly question one time. "Don't you feel the need for some clerical help?"

"What for?" she asked with a smile.

In addition to these daily tasks, she speaks all over the world, has several books on the best-seller list, and yet never misses my birthday. (I suspect scores of others find Barbara faithfully acknowledging their birthdays as well.)

One of the patterns we Joyful Journey speakers have established after a conference is to gather on Saturday evening, order room service, eat, laugh, and debrief. It's a great way to bring closure to the weekend and to share with one another the various ways we watched God reveal himself to the dear women in attendance.

At the conclusion of one of our festive debriefings, I was especially weary. I even pondered sliding over to the right lane. But Barbara was animatedly chatting and showing no sign of fatigue. I knew she had risen several hours before I had that morning. She and Bill always go over to the conference site early so they can make their "splashes of joy" rocks available to the eager women who love taking these brightly colored little reminders home with them. I watched her now, still zipping along in the fast lane, and was filled yet again with admiration. I thought, *Marilyn, you will have to really floorboard the gas pedal to ever catch up with that sweetheart.*

While I try to at least keep Barbara in sight as she and I bolt our way through the rapid completion of our tasks, I must confess I often become impatient with those who get in my way and barely move. This is one negative effect of a fast-lane mentality.

For example, last week I made what I expected to be a quick trip to the supermarket with the intention of buying a few necessary items. I planned to zip through the express checkout lane. (Whoever came up with that concept is my kind of person!)

Unfortunately, I fell victim to a dawdling cart pusher in a narrow aisle in front of me. I was trapped into witnessing her heady dilemma of whether to buy mushrooms with stems, mushrooms in pieces, or to go the deluxe route and purchase the mushroom caps. I found myself with nearly murderous impulses as she slowly and deliberately read the description of each can's contents. She seemed oblivious to my toe tapping, and so I finally said, "Excuse me. If you don't mind, could you move your cart just a little? I'd like to get by."

Still unaware of my presence, she returned all the cans to the shelf and resumed her laborious journey down the aisle. Finally, I spotted a passing zone, careened around her, and flashed over to the soft drinks aisle.

On my way to the express lane, I remembered I needed bread. I backtracked quickly to the bread aisle only to find the label-reader absorbed in the claims of the "new and better" blueberry Pop-Tarts.

As I drove home, I thought, *Marilyn, what's your story? Why on earth do you get so agitated over those slower than you? You experience the same reaction when a car gets in front of you and has the audacity to go the speed limit. What's your deal? Well, I'll tell you, Precious, I think you're doing what Patsy calls "sportin' a 'tude."* In spite of that crabby self-talk, I totally agreed with myself. I did have a 'tude I needed to look at.

I decided to get down to business and work on this. As I thought about it, I realized that, while I think of God as a pretty efficient guy, he doesn't always operate in the fast lane. He operates quite slowly, in fact, when he needs to. Sometimes he has to, not because of his style, but because of mine. My reluctance, my resistance, my disobedience frequently get in the way of my progress and growth. My reluctance to be still and know that he is God; my resistance to hearing his voice when I don't like what he is saying; my disobedience in pretending I didn't hear him in the first place. He has to wait for me all the time ... not to accomplish the tasks in my life but to accommodate his Spirit in my soul. And yet, what is so mind-boggling is his patience with my slowness to learn, slowness to yield, slowness to obey. Second Chronicles 30:9 reads, "The LORD your God is gracious and merciful, and will not turn away his face from you" (KJV).

God would wait for years behind the mushroom-Pop-Tart lady if it took that long to get her attention. And he does the same for me. He doesn't toe-tap behind me. He doesn't go careening past me, having lost all patience with my heady dilemmas. In fact, he invites me to share my dilemmas with him. "Let him have all your worries and cares, for he is always thinking about you and watching everything that concerns you" (1 Peter 5:7 TLB).

I'm also told I am to love as he loves. Listen to this verse: "May God who gives patience, steadiness, and encouragement help you to live in complete harmony with each other—each with the attitude of Christ toward the other" (Rom. 15:5 TLB). I guess that means my 'tude for every slow-walking, slow-talking, and slow-driving person on the face of the earth is to be one of Christlike patience and loving acceptance. That's a divine mandate—it's also a tall order.

As always, when I'm called to a behavior or attitude that is higher than my humanness, I'm comforted when I remember that it is not I, but he, who loves through me. Nevertheless, I need to get in concert with him, and that means that my humanness must cooperate with his divineness.

That being the case, I came up with a plan for those times when I need to exhibit my "Christ-'tude." It was simply this: The moment someone slowed me down or cut me off, rather than yield to my often uncharitable thoughts, I would instead pray for that person. I would pray for his or her family, job, health, and general well-being. I would commit to the Lord that person's challenges and hurts, and I would pray for his or her salvation.

This plan seems like it might be a workable one, but it's still new to me. So far I've had only one opportunity to put it into action.

This morning I stopped to fill up the car's tank. A number of vehicles were in front of me, which was no surprise. This particular station has the lowest prices in Palm Desert, so there's always a bit of a wait.

I accommodated the idea of a wait, but I soon experienced some 'tude trouble with the guy in the car in front of me. When his turn came to tank up, instead of moving to the first pump (both the first and second pumps became available at the same time), he remained at the third pump. My very reasonable thought was, *If you moved up to the first pump, I could use the second one, and the person behind me could use the third.*

Apparently that never occurred to this self-absorbed fellow. I couldn't back up and swing around to one of the other pumps because of the car behind me. So I sat there and could feel that very familiar creeping anxiety—I wanted to be in the fast lane while stalled by circumstances beyond my control in the slow lane. Rather than let this person inordinately annoy me, I studied him instead. (I momentarily forgot I was supposed to pray for him.)

I noted his meticulously combed hair, which he had sprayed into symmetrical position. He wore a pressed light blue suit with the starched white shirt open casually at the neck revealing a tanned chest upon which nestled one thin gold chain. (I haven't seen a chain on a man in a long time. Was he out of style?) I also noticed his impeccably polished shoes above which occasionally flashed his blue socks, the same color blue as the suit. (I thought socks were supposed to match the shoes, not the suit . . .) *I don't think I'd feel bad if you dribbled gas on your shiny shoes, fella.* I thought. *I don't even think I'd feel bad if a low-flying bird dropped a deposit in your pretty hair.* Oh, no, I was supposed to be praying for this guy, not slipping into one of my 'tudes!

By now he was carefully cleaning his windshield. Reluctantly (I didn't really think he deserved prayer), I began to pray for the possible concerns and burdens in his life, for his health, for his family, for the events facing him this particular day, and then, very tenderly with a spirit other than mine, I prayed for his salvation. I prayed that the Holy Spirit would so penetrate this man's consciousness that he would feel the touch of God upon him all day.

I soon discovered how this kind of praying could quell my rising tide of resentment. By the time he finally finished grooming his car, I felt so tender toward him, had he not driven away, I might have embarrassed myself by running over and hugging him.

I plan to try this prayer response again. I like the way it kept my fast-lane brain productively involved while my body idled around, waiting for the chance to speed up. It kept my emotions from zooming out of control, and it kept my heart purring along in a sweet state. And it did the guy some good, too.

If your love is for the left lane, swing on over there and feel the wind flying through your hair, and the bugs spatting against your dark glasses. But if the right lane beckons you, indulge your penchant for counting wildflowers in the field or discarded tennis shoes on the freeway. Most important, we must all remember, left-laners or right-laners, we are to be tender with each other, patient with each other, kind to each other, and above all, we are to pray for each other. I learned all this sitting at the gas pump—in life's slow lane.

Eleven

Under Construction

Barbara Johnson

Drive carefully! Remember, it's not only a car that can be recalled by its maker.

—ANONYMOUS

The road sign "Under Construction" stirs up a memory that is embedded like shrapnel in my heart. Many years ago my husband, Bill, was seriously injured when he hit some debris on a mountain road. As a result, our lives took a major turn.

The young people of our church had planned a retreat, and Bill and I had offered to be counselors. That afternoon before the retreat, I wound my way up the mountain road taking food and supplies to the retreat center. I was to drive back home for supper, and then later in the evening I would return to the retreat center with the children. Bill would take more supplies up before I made my final trip.

As I returned from my afternoon trip, I came to a place where the road was under construction. Big warning signs were posted, and a construction worker was letting the cars through a large section of the road one at a time with a long wait in between. Even though it was a warm April day, only a few cars were using the road because it wasn't open to the public yet after the heavy winter rains. As I sat in the car waiting my turn to maneuver through the construction area, I remember thinking, *I must be sure to tell Bill about this debris in the road.* When he drove up the road in the dark later, no flagman would be there to help him through the torn-up area.

After I arrived home from the mountain trip, I hurriedly prepared supper while Bill packed his supplies. With all the commotion of getting the kids ready, I forgot to tell him to watch for the roadwork.

Later that night, as I entered the construction area, I came upon a man lying in the middle of the road, covered with blood, sand, and glass. The highway department had left plenty of debris in the road, unaware any motorists would be using this road at night. There were no warning signs, and no flagman was available to help drivers navigate the dug-up road. Bill had run into the debris.

His accident was only the first of a number of traumas we would face in the next nine years of our lives. With Bill near death and our family seeming to disintegrate before our eyes, we had entered a rough, debris-strewn road that would test the mettle of our vehicle of faith.

One immediate test would be to face the aftermath of Bill's accident. My thoughts returned repeatedly to the same litany: If only I had told him about the construction. If only I had prepared him for the debris on the road. If only I had remembered to say, "Be careful—the road is under construction." If only . . . these two words spun around in my head like a never-ending, horrible carnival ride.

Sometimes we drain ourselves of energy and whip ourselves with guilt using the two words, "If only." But in God's economy things happen all the time that remind us we are under construction and still imperfect. We make mistakes. Like the little slogan says, "Be patient with me, God is not finished with me yet."

I've heard it said that patience is the ability to idle your motor when you feel like stripping your gears. We appreciate it when others idle their motors in the face of our imperfections. I needed to be patient with myself, to accept myself in my failure to mention the road construction.

Bill and I certainly had the opportunity to practice patience when our son Barney and his wife bought a repossessed house near our home. Barney didn't know much about repairs and would often call Bill to come over to "help" him. The house, empty for three years and with no one in attendance, was in bad shape.

One day Barney called with an urgent request. Someone who had lived there previously had shoved rocks, if you can imagine, down the sink and garbage disposal. Bill took all the plumbing apart and pulled out the rocks and gravel. Finally, after hours of work, the plumbing was functioning again.

Barney had no training in brickwork, yet decided one day to cover one entire end of his house with bricks. He had mixed the cement himself. By the time we arrived to admire his handiwork, all the bricks had slid south into a huge pile. Evidently he hadn't used the proper mixture for the cement.

Several years have passed since then, and Barney has moved to Reno where he does wonderful brickwork, specializing in patios and ornamental work. He took us up to the big Harrah's once and showed us the magnificent rock fountain he had created there, complete with flowers and water flowing in various directions determined by the shapes of the concrete stones Barney had made. How much he had learned, grown, changed, and developed from that day all of his bricks had sunk into a pile.

As humans, we, too, are under construction. Our early responses to challenges to our faith are imperfect and uncertain, but as we grow we learn we can trust our Father, who has guided us through many construction zones.

A cartoon I saw recently showed a couple in a car coming upon a road sign reading, "Highway of Life. Construction Zone Next Forty Years." Isn't that just how it is—constant changes, detours, something being built as something else is being torn down. Life is never a done deal; it's never perfect. And it will never be perfect in this broken, mixed-up world. There isn't a perfect anything. The perfect picture hasn't been painted, the perfect poem hasn't been written, and the perfect song hasn't been sung. Everything in the world remains to be done over and done better.

My friend Lynda has looked really sharp lately, and when I complimented her, she said she had bought a new bra. Its name? "Nobody's Perfect."

So here we are, waiting for the perfect soap, the perfect bra, the perfect cosmetic to correct our imperfections.

I was at the car wash recently where I saw a little spray bottle with a label that said, "New Car Smell." An illustration of a spanking new car wrapped with a big red bow leapt out from the label. I figured my 1987 Volvo could stand a new car smell, so I bought the little bottle and sprayed it all around inside the car. Then I almost got sick from the odor—a blend of old oil, tar, and a hint of banana. If a new car really smelled like *that*, I'm sure the owner would demand a refund. But I had wrongly assumed I could "fix" my imperfect old car with a simple spray. Some of us are easily fooled by signs and advertisements that promise us everything will be wonderful.

Some years ago, when stores started carrying unpopped popcorn in bright red, green, purple, and orange, we eagerly bought it and took it home to pop it. We all stood around and watched it popping, expecting to see this wonderful assortment of colors, but to our dismay, the popcorn came out plain white as usual. The colors we anticipated failed to materialize.

A friend of mine, Sarah, sent away for some marvelous stuff advertised on TV called "Dream Away." You were instructed to take these pills at night, and in the morning when you awoke, you would have dreamed away your fat. Within a few nights of pleasant dreaming, you would be slim and lovely. You know the saying, "If it's too good to be true, it probably isn't."

So we learn that no spray can make an old car smell new, no advertisement will turn white popcorn into colored, and no dreams will reduce our fat cells. Still, we long for those quick miracles.

We live in a world under construction, and the people in it are full of quirks with homes full of imperfections. One friend of mine scrimped and saved to buy some expensive wallpaper for her son's bedroom. It was so costly, it had to be special ordered. When the call came that it had finally arrived, she was thrilled and hurried to the store to get it and bring it home. The next day her husband wanted to surprise her, so while she was out shopping, he laboriously papered the bedroom. The colorful balloons on the wallpaper had strings hanging down from them so each balloon seemed to soar in the sky. But her husband made a huge mistake. He put the wallpaper on upside down so that the strings ran up the wall like slithering snakes rather than hang gracefully down as intended. She had anticipated a perfect room, but she ended up with just the opposite.

Learning to live with upside-down situations isn't easy. But we all must, since mistakes, things under construction, and imperfect or unfinished situations and people are all around us.

The need to adjust to imperfections is reinforced by the clock in our car. It's one hour off from October to April when the time changes. The mechanism is broken so we always have to subtract an hour if we want to know the true time. Perhaps this is teaching me something—that I should soon purchase another car with a working clock (hope, hope!). More likely I'm learning that some things in life will never be what they should be. We'll always need to fix, mend, repair, renovate—or adjust. As the sign in my kitchen says, "Home Sweet Home—Learn to Adjust."

As Christians we know we are only pilgrims here, not settlers. That helps us to adjust and gives everything a new color. We are in transition, in change, in a state of flux. We will never have it completely together—until we get to glory!

But the torn-up road ahead can take its toll. It truly is a toll road, taking its wear and tear on our very souls.

A package arrived on my doorstep recently marked, "Damaged in transit but deliverable." A string hung off one corner, the address label was torn into several pieces, and some audiotapes hung out of another corner. I wondered if an elephant had tap-danced on this package. "Who says this pile of cardboard is 'deliverable'?" I asked the postman.

I thought of how many lives like mine are damaged and hurt. They *should* be marked, "Fragile. Handle with Care." We are all like packages on a long journey. The pain of losing a child, the heartache of the loss of a dear one, or the pain of physical disability may have crushed us. We may feel that we, too, have been trampled by elephants.

Instead of being handled like fine china, we are slammed from one side to another, battered and scarred by life's journey. We are damaged in transit. We become unraveled, unglued, undone, and begin to come apart at all corners.

I was speaking to a women's group recently, and one gal approached me after the meeting. "I enjoyed hearing you," she said, "because you aren't wrapped too tight!" I didn't know if she meant I was falling apart like a ball of yarn with all the knots showing or if she was simply appreciative of my often lighthearted approach to life. Yes, I have been on a long, hard journey, shoved against the walls of despair and frustration, handled carelessly with no thought for the fragile and often broken heart inside that needs no more crushing. But even though I may be damaged in transit, after all the rough handling and construction in my life, I will be claimed by the Master.

I am learning to lay down my agonies and pick up my credentials as I continue on the journey—regardless of the Under Construction areas. There is no instant glory; there is no microwave maturity. The journey for most of us is a long one, but we can support each other along the way. We are not isolated. We are all on the same trip; some are simply farther down the road. And we will all arrive to be claimed by the Lord as part of his family. No unclaimed freight in this bunch!

Now, it seems that some of us think glory won't be all that glorious so we need to add to it. I heard a story once about a rich man who was determined to "take it all with him" when he died, and he prayed to that end until finally the Lord gave in. There was just one condition: He could bring only one suitcase of his wealth. The rich man decided to fill the case with gold bullion. Then the day came when God called him home. St. Peter greeted him at heaven's gate but told him he couldn't bring his suitcase.

"Oh, but I have an agreement with God," the man explained.

"That's unusual," said St. Peter. "Mind if I take a look?"

The man opened the suitcase to reveal the shining gold bullion. St. Peter was amazed. "Why in the world would you bring pavement up here?" The man hadn't realized that the streets of heaven were paved in gold.

At some point during my school days I decided that *pavement* was one of the most soothing sounding words I'd ever heard. We think of "paving the way," how God paves our path before us. Smooth Road Ahead could be posted on any newly paved road. What a joy to "sail" through life on smooth pavement.

Of course, smooth pavement in our imperfect world isn't always a good sign. I've heard it said that the road to ruin always seems in good repair. I saw a Ziggy cartoon once where a man told him, "The human body is the Lord's temple, Mr. Ziggy, but yours is in serious danger of being torn down to make way for a parking lot."

In actuality, smooth pavement is not what awaits us on the road ahead; snarling ruts, piled-up debris, serious bumps, and gooey tar does. Sometimes construction takes the form of those awful what-if questions like those with which I tormented myself after Bill's accident. We blame ourselves and others for old mistakes and sins that God has long ago forgotten.

Are you letting the sorrow and the what-ifs of life rob you of the joy of what is? We need to continue on, to drive through the construction with our hearts set on seeing what it is that God is doing *in* us as we drive *through* the hurt.

A friend of mine claims we need bumpers—angel bumpers—on our cars to protect us from serious damage. Psalm 34:7 says, "The angel of the LORD encampeth round about them that fear him, and delivereth them" (KJV). Sounds like an angel bumper to me. My friend also suggests we equip ourselves with the shock absorber of laughter to make the journey easier and the windshield wipers of God's love to swish away the what-ifs so we can more clearly see what is.

I remember the little plaque that hung in our home as I grew up: "Only one life, 'twill soon be past. Only what's done for Christ will last." Those words help me keep perspective when I find I am in a construction zone with lots of delays and lots of debris scattered in my way. Think about it—we are here for such a short time, yet what we do here is for eternity. Heaven is our final home, and while we can't take gold bullion or anything else with us, we can send some things on ahead. The love we lavish on those in need will yield results that last forever. So let's marinate folks in love.

Once we comprehend the brevity of life here and the importance of eternity with him, everything falls into place. God is in charge of it all. Someone has said the reason we don't have to worry about tomorrow is because God is already there. Our final travel arrangements are made, reservations are confirmed, and it's all first class (John 14:2). As for passports, we will only be permitted past the gates if we have proper credentials and if our names are registered with the ruling Authority (Rev. 21:27). Our ticket is a written pledge (John 5:24). No baggage will be allowed, and we must leave behind all of the bewilderment, shame, despair, guilt, and fear we regularly carry around. There will be no need for vaccinations because all diseases are unknown at our destination (Rev. 21:4). The exact departure date has not been announced; travelers are advised to prepare to leave on short notice (1 Thess. 5:1–2).

That's why it's best to hold loosely the earthly things on this journey—our kids, our jobs, our homes, our security—because we are just traveling through. Our final destination, after we make it through the construction zones, will be so glorious, it will be worth everything we've gone through. Earth, with all its imperfections, has no sorrow that heaven cannot heal.

Twelve

Men at Work

Luci Swindoll

Good company in a journey makes the way to seem the shorter.

—Izaak Walton

I remember a gift my dad gave me when I was about twelve. It was a toolbox. We'd had trouble with the toilet overflowing and stopping up, all at varying times and to varying degrees, and I wanted to fix it. So did Dad.

He knew I was fascinated with any kind of repair or rebuilding work, and so whenever the toilet started acting up, he would get out his toolbox, invite me to come along, and together we would set out to correct the problem. He would supply the labor, and I would supply the questions: "What's that rubber thing? Why's that chain loose and kinda floppin' around? Isn't that little black gadget supposed to stay put?"

Daddy would respond patiently to each question, explaining what he was doing and why, always with this concluding statement: "You know you've fixed it when the dingfod bumps up against the tootnanny and squirts the affidavit through the lolly-gog." Then we would leave the bathroom smiling, thinking this toilet would work perfectly until the millennium. This was the only bathroom in the house, and it had to stay in good working order.

The day came, however, when our toilet seemed to be on its last gurgle. It had developed some sort of mechanical death rattle, making little spitting and dripping sounds. Even jiggling the flush handle didn't alter the problem now. It was driving us all crazy.

So, after school one day, I spotted Daddy hard at work, his head half buried in the toilet tank. As always, I went into the bathroom to watch him work. When he saw me, he stood up, reached behind the bathroom door, and pulled out a little toolbox, half the size of his. I opened it to find a number of miniature tools just for me.

I was out of my head with joy. This was *my* toolbox. I thanked him over and over, and then he showed me how to use each one of those tools.

He taught me about being patient and taking my time with each job. He pointed out each of the toilet's parts, calling them by their proper names: the float ball, the lift chain, the tank ball, the trip lever, and so on. This time I worked beside him, installing a new part here and there until we had finished the job.

Upon completion, we stood over the toilet bowl, pulled the flush handle, and stared into the depths of the water as it swished down the trap and out the waste pipe. We looked at each other, grinned, and shook hands. The tootnanny was definitely squirting the affidavit through the lollygog, and we were sharing the joy of a job well done. I don't remember that toilet ever giving us trouble again.

It's fun to recall stories about my father. In fact, when I think of him, I often become wistfully nostalgic. He was a Man at Work in my life, teaching me so much more than I realized at the time.

My mind can quickly conjure up clear pictures of him: handsome, dapper, and socially engaging. Daddy was a tall man with a strong, commanding voice but with soft blue eyes and an even softer heart. He was kind, funny, wise, and encouraging—all the things I like in a person.

Whenever I got in trouble as a little girl, I rarely went to Mother for reconciliation. I went to my dad because he always received me without judgment or criticism. Oh, he would discipline me, but even that was done with a little lecture on "it's the principle of the thing" first and the rod afterward.

As a college student, I received letters twice weekly from Daddy. They were full of Scripture, encouraging comments, and questions about what I was learning and doing. He didn't bother telling me of the late-breaking news on Quince Street; he was too busy offering me his love and prayers. (The local and neighborhood news came from Mother's letters: ". . . Your father went to the coast this past Monday with Mr. Roberts, and they caught a mess of fish," or, "We had a minor accident in the old Ford. Had to take it in for repair," or, "Your dad got a promotion with a raise. Isn't that nice?")

As I think back, I remember that he sometimes used rhymes to convey his thoughts. It was fun for him, and he did it well. And I loved it. I was a captive audience.

Unwittingly, my dad set the standard for all the men I've encountered since. While I realize that I will never find another like him, several men have been at work in my life, communicating encouragement in a hundred different and appreciated ways. God has taught me a lot about himself through these men. Fortunately, I have always had positive, healthy relationships with those of the opposite sex, and because of this my relationship with God has also been healthy. I was treated right by them. Why shouldn't I be treated right by him? I figured if I could trust men, I could trust God as well. This has been an enormous blessing in my life, and I'm grateful for it.

As a single person, I appreciate that God has given me meaningful friendships with men of all ages and at every stage of life. In so doing, he has taught me his love, shown me his grace, and provided me a place of spiritual community.

Now, families have built-in relationships that God can use to develop character in the lives of its members. This is a by-product of the family unit. But, as a single, I must take the time and energy to cultivate these relationships. I can't afford to live in the world isolated from the input and friendship of others: married or unmarried, men or women, children or seniors, ethnic or Anglo, rich or poor, educated or uneducated. It behooves me as a follower of Jesus Christ both to teach and to learn from the community in which God has placed me and called me to accountability.

A big part of that community are my siblings—two wonderful brothers. They are both in public Christian ministry and are a constant source of encouragement to me in one way or another. As children, naturally, at times they tried my patience or tested my faith, but as I look back from this vantage point, I see that even those moments were of God's design. A family of five living in a small house has difficulty simply managing the close quarters without the daily urge to kill. Upon reflection, I laugh when I think about our circus times together as youngsters.

But it is really only now that I'm older and aware of each brother's intangible gift of encouragement that I can see God at work in me through them. For example, I have boxes of letters my younger brother, Chuck, has written me over the years. There must be hundreds, and I've saved them all. Letters full of appreciation, affirmation, and cheerfulness—either opening or ending with Scriptures of encouragement and blessing.

Just for fun, I reread some of Chuck's letters the other day. The following was written thirty-eight years ago while Chuck was in the Marine Corps on the island of Okinawa, and I was living in Texas. It arrived just a few days before my birthday.

May this birthday (your 26th) be thoroughly enjoyable and unforgettable. I tried to buy a large box, large enough for me to get in and be mailed to you on your birthday but had no luck! Since I cannot be with you (oh, how I wish I could), I'm sending all my love in a small gift coming with this, hoping that every time you wear it, you will remember the love I have for you, the greatest, sweetest, and most beautiful sister in the whole world. Happy birthday, my dear . . . have a great one!

If that doesn't warm a sister's heart, nothing does. Earlier in that letter Chuck admitted how lonesome he was, being so far away from his "group" (as he called his wife, family, and friends), and how he was looking forward to the day he would come home.

But he never seemed to feel sorry for himself. Immediately after acknowledging his loneliness, he would follow up with something upbeat or encouraging.

I firmly believe the greatest lessons are learned while we are apart from every single one of our loved ones, friends and groups, and are forced to consider him . . . his guidance, his grace, his love, his Word . . . What constant assurance is afforded those who "trust in the Lord forever," for in him is everlasting strength.

Week after week I would read those letters from a man so far away from everyone he held dear, and I would find new strength for my own burdens, light for my own pathway, encouragement to press on. I feel that same strength even now, as I reread this old, yellowed letter that I treasure like pure gold. The same words of comfort and cheer apply today, just as they did almost four decades ago.

More recently, Chuck and I discussed tithing—the act of tithing in general and my lack of tithing in particular. I had felt for some time that I was being negligent in this spiritual discipline. I more or less confessed this to Chuck, knowing full well he and

Cynthia had faithfully tithed all of their married lives and that they put a high premium on their financial commitment to the Lord. I had been afraid to mention it to Chuck since he was not only my brother and friend, but my pastor. It was just that I felt this niggling so often in my heart I thought I might as well ask for his counsel. Mind you, he had never talked with me about tithing prior to this occasion, nor has he ever questioned anything about the integrity of my spiritual walk.

After I told him how I felt, he didn't chide me. He simply asked, "And why don't you tithe, sis? What's keeping you from it?"

"Well," I said, "I'm afraid I'll run out of money. There's nobody there to bail me out if I can't meet my financial commitments. I mean, what happens if I run out of money before I run out of month?"

He kind of smiled, and with all the grace in the world and those warm eyes of his, he said, "Sis, everything you have is God's—your work, your health, your money, your life. You can't outdo or second-guess God. Why don't you try tithing and just see what happens? I promise you, you're in for a surprise."

We were both silent for a moment as I let his suggestion sink in. Then he added, "And, Sis, anybody can tithe ten percent. Give more than that. Trust God for more than that."

"Okay, eleven," I countered. "How about eleven percent?"

He nodded. "That's good. Eleven is a good start. Now, you commit to that off the gross of every dollar you make, and watch God work. You'll never run out of money."

Well, as it turns out, my brother knew what he was talking about. I am truly amazed at what I've seen God do since that day I made a commitment to tithe. After I decided wall's down, roof's off to trust God no matter what, he has brought an increase I never dreamed possible. Time after time after time. Never have I run out of money. In fact, on the contrary, I've earned more money than ever before, and each year I've increased my tithe by at least one or two percent. Through my brother God began to show me a side of his grace I had never known, because I had never trusted him that much before. In some aspect, I always held back; I wanted to be the one in control of my finances. Now I don't wait. I really believe God will do what he says.

Chuck's encouraging words, "You will never run out," motivated me to step out in faith with a new reliance on the Lord. And as I took this step, I found it easier to trust God in other ways. When we experience his provision of a promise in one area, it does become easier to trust him in another area. Then another. And another.

Why is it that we limit God? He generally isn't the one who puts the skids on our hopes and dreams. We do it ourselves. We think, *I'm too old*, or *I'm not good enough*, or *What will people think?* or *I've never done this before*, or *I can't afford it*. So we don't even move off home plate. We simply strike out at bat.

The truth is we can't accomplish what is set before us . . . in and of ourselves. It's best to admit that as soon as possible and then turn our thoughts to this: God is all powerful, and he can do anything. I've tried to crank out so many things in my own strength, never inviting God into the project, and it's absolute *work*—stressful, tiring—even boring. But every time I turn loose of my control and trust God at a deeper level, I learn just a bit more about what God wants to do for me.

A couple of years ago I bought an expensive computer that could perform a variety of fancy functions. Actually, my elder brother, Orville (the family genius), bought all the parts, with my permission and money, of course, then carried it on the plane from Miami to Los Angeles in six or eight enormous boxes, and finally assembled it in my condo in Palm Desert. It's fantastic, able to do many things I have yet to learn. Every day, even now, I spend time stretching my mind and limited talents at the keyboard.

When prodded by my brother, I could have said, "No, there's no way at the age of sixty-three I'm going to bite off the task of learning the ABCs of DOS. I'm too old for that." Instead, I've decided to learn all I can, and through trial and error and Orville's constant encouragement (he's only an e-mail or phone call away), I'm getting better as the months go by.

I recently hit a major technical snag, though, and was frothing at the mouth about this high-powered machine. *Why did I ever buy it in the first place?* I muttered as I put in a distress call to Orville. After I explained my dilemma, he agreed it was kind of a mess. But he walked me through the problem, and an hour later I was back on track. As I thanked him for helping his "old" sister, who is getting senile, he simply laughed. "Sis," he said, "would you rather be fighting a computer problem that takes a little figuring out, or lying in a nursing home, waiting for the attendant to come down the hall with your ground-up food?" Okay, okay, I love my computer; I *love* it.

I think maybe Marilyn should be writing this chapter because three of the most prominent men in her life have been the same "men at work" in mine: her husband, Ken; her son, Jeff; and her son-in-law, Steve.

Dr. Kenneth Meberg (who died in 1990 of pancreatic cancer) was one outstanding person. He was brilliant, kindhearted, caring, and terribly funny. His death at the age of fifty-two stunned us all, but the legacy of encouragement and kindness he extended toward me will never die. I feel it every day. He offered me good advice and wise counsel time and time again whenever I went to him with concerns about my work or my future. He was unbiased, knowledgeable, and could see through the guff to the real issues of life. He was complimentary and a delight to be around. The world suffered a great loss at his untimely death.

The Mebergs were hospitable and inclusive in their outreach to extended family, friends, and neighbors, and they often had dinner parties at which I was a frequent guest. One evening as I found myself once again the recipient of their hospitality and Ken's culinary prowess, the thought hit me that more often than not I had my feet under Ken's table as the benefactor of his generosity and kindness. I suddenly felt unworthy or perhaps somewhat of a taker.

In an effort to show my appreciation, I tossed out, "You know, Ken, if you had to pay for this, it would really cost you." Of course, the minute the words fell from my lips, I immediately realized I'd expressed myself all wrong. What I meant was . . . But it was too late.

Ken threw back his head in a hearty laugh. From that moment on, this line became a joke between us. We used it on countless occasions to tease one another.

The year before Ken died, I was invited to speak on a Caribbean cruise to a group of singles. When I learned we needed two speakers instead of one, I invited Marilyn to share the podium with me and included her family as my guests. We had an unforgettable time. And wouldn't you know, right in the middle of an elegant shipboard meal, Ken whispered in my ear, "You know, Luci, if you had to pay for this, it would really cost you." Indeed. And if I had to pay for the laughter, joy, and spirited conversation I exchanged with Ken in those years, it would cost more than I had.

Men at Work. Ken's son, Jeff, is such a chip off the old block. Funny, enterprising, protective, responsible. The kid is a riot but so kind. I remember the evening, about four years ago, he called me and asked if he could take me to lunch the next day. Thrilled, I assured him I would love to be his "date." (Jeff is actually married to a beautiful woman, Carla, to whom I introduced him in 1988.)

He picked me up the next day and took me to one of my favorite restaurants in Orange County. "Luci, I want to tell you something," he said as we ate. "I'm glad we could have lunch so we'd have a nice setting in which I could present this idea." Needless to say, my curiosity was piqued.

"Carla and I have been talking," he went on, "and we want you to know that if you ever get tired of speaking or writing and decide it's time to relax for the rest of your life, we'd like for you to move in with us. We want to take care of you when you get old. We don't want you to have to worry about money or illness or any of those things. You can just live at our house, and we'll meet your needs. In fact, we'd love it if my mom would live there, too."

I broke down and cried. I had known and loved this young man since he was seven years old. Now here he was, all grown up, happily married and in a job he loved, asking me to put up my feet and relax at his expense for the rest of my life. I could hardly stand the joy and complete peace I found in his invitation. Whether or not it ever comes to pass remains to be seen, but that's not what matters to me. What matters is that he thought of it and set up a special time to present it to me. This kind of kindness I will never forget.

Jeff is such a special person. I can't count the times he has cooked for me, in both my kitchen and his. Marilyn's son-in-law, Steve, is also an incredible cook. (The best cooks I've known are all men.)

One Thanksgiving I invited about a dozen friends to my home for the big festivities, and I was amused to see the men taking over my kitchen: Jeff, Steve, Kurt Ratican, and Julius Karoblis (the latter two could open their own gourmet restaurant). As the women in the group sat outside sipping Perrier and enjoying hors d'oeuvres, we watched the men through the sliding glass door, literally "at work" in my kitchen. A couple of them even wore aprons. They conversed with one another about hockey, football, or work, while madly discussing how long to sauté the mushrooms and how often to baste the turkey. What a meal, cooked to perfection by the men in our lives.

One other man deserves honorable mention as a fellow at work in my life. Well, one could hardly call him a man yet, but he's getting there. He is Marilyn's grandson, Ian Kenneth Soule. Ian, at fourteen months old, works on me in ways that no other male has in years. What am I to do? When I go into a baby shop, my hand heads straight for my checkbook to buy him "a little something to wear." If I know I'm going to see him soon, my camera begins quietly chanting, "You need more film; you need more film."

Ian is capable of reducing my normal use of the English language to a baby babble that only he and I can understand. Singing opera in the shower turns into soft lullabies. Is there a cure for this malady? I think not!

The best part of all is that Ian does nothing whatsoever to deserve this attention except be himself. He doesn't intentionally perform, and he doesn't make good grades; he cries and frets and pouts and creates messes of almost everything he touches. In fact, Ian is *work*. But I love him to pieces.

Thank goodness, there is no cure for my malady. Ian brings out the vulnerability in me that I see in him. He is helpless before me, looking to me to accept and love him, no matter what he does.

Isn't that the way the Lord loves us? He doesn't expect us to perform for him. He loves us always—when we're disappointed or hurt or making a mess of things. Sometimes we speak to him in a language that only he can understand. What matters to him is that we are vulnerable, that we are completely ourselves. We are work, too, but God cherishes us.

Who are the men in your life that God uses to meet your emotional and spiritual needs? Do you treasure them? Do you tell them so? Do you encourage them in return? This is so important for all women to do, but especially for the single woman who can easily become jaded because she hasn't found the man of her dreams or discouraged because it feels as if life has passed her by. It's all too easy to get down and *stay* down.

Every now and then, show yourself a mental video of the Men at Work in your life: men in your family, among your friends, in your workplace or your church, men who have treated you with dignity and kindness when you needed it most. I'm not referring to romance here, but the relationships that are helping to form your outlook and *in look* on life.

As I reflect on the Men at Work in my life (and there are so many others I could have written about), I realize God is the one who has done the most work through the years. He has woven all these individuals in and out of my life, revealing himself through them. Starting with my father when I was a little girl and continuing to this present day, he uses these gentle men to demonstrate his wisdom, kindness, provision, humor, and encouragement. And he who began a good work in me will continue it (Phil. 1:6).

Thirteen

Duck Crossing

Patsy Clairmont

"Glorious, stirring sight!" murmured Toad, never offering to move. "The poetry of motion!"

—KENNETH GRAHAME, *WIND IN THE WILLOWS*

I live in a storybook kind of town, with lampposts, church bells, horse-drawn carriage rides, and a children's park called the Imagination Station. In the center of town is a scenic millpond where one can find a gazebo, bridges, summer concerts, and a gazillion ducks. You can see folks toting bags of bread and popcorn as offerings and bribes for our bobbing bird population. From the toddler to great gramps, people from all over come to feed the ducks and geese of Brighton.

An official Duck Crossing sign is posted on Main Street, near the pond. This is because quite regularly the ducks sashay across the road. *Sashay* might be misleading in that it suggests steady movement. What really happens is that the ducks amble out to the middle of the road, where they are struck with a bolt of indecisiveness. They then waddle joyfully back and forth across the center line keeping traffic stopped in both directions. If you honk to encourage a decision, they often take a what's-a-matter-with-you stance. They stretch their necks and tilt their heads slightly to one side, as if to say, "Don't get your feathers in an uproar, bub."

These procrastinating preeners parade pompously through our little city both to the pleasure and perplexity of the towns-people. For along their webbed journeys they leave . . . residue. Generous residue. Green (yuk) residue. I think you get the picture, and it ain't all pretty. But even with the ducks' telltale offerings, our community not only tolerates them, but finds them endearing.

Get this: These iridescent featherheads have been designated town mascot. You'll even find we've emblazoned them on sweat-shirts boasting our city's name. Now isn't that just ducky.

I have learned from observing our town mascot that ducks are not known for their brilliance. My neighbor Alicia was clean-ing out her garage one day when she found an old damp blue tarp. She decided to let it dry in the sun, so she spread it out on the grass. A short time later she heard an unusual honking sound com-ing from her backyard. Mr. and Mrs. Daffy Duck had made a three-point landing beside the tarp thinking it was a private pond with their name on it. Alicia consoled the misguided pair as she pointed out that the tarp was not even a small puddle. (I think the feath-erbrains are still in therapy after that jolting revelation.)

I've noticed that some curious folks have ducklike qualities: indecisive, looking for a handout, residuers, misguided, and on the verge of quacking up. Oh, my, I think I've just described my menopausal self. Since entering estrogen poverty I haven't been sashaying through life as I once did. I've definitely been struck with a bolt of indecisiveness. I now have trouble with major decisions: Should I brush my teeth first or wash my face? Should I wear pantyhose today or knee-highs? These mental stumbling blocks can slow down one's day, not to mention one's productivity.

As if cranial constipation isn't restrictive enough, I find I'm constantly begging others for, not popcorn or dry bread crumbs (if you put peanut butter-marshmallow on them I might accept), but for air. "Please kick up the air conditioner. On high—now. Fresh air—cold air—just give me air. I can't help it if it's winter, just put the dad-blame thing on. Thank you!"

Some women beg for cash flow, I just want air flow. Without cool air I'm afraid one day Les will wake up and find a pile of ashes where I once lay. In the night I will have burnt to a crisp from one too many hot flashes.

Then there's the residue. Gratefully, I'm in between a need for diapers and Depends (of course we know which one I'm closest to). But the residue I'm most guilty of depositing is verbiage. If one word will do, I feel led to release ten. I don't know where all these words come from, but they tend to spill out like an oil slick, and we know how that can stick to one's feathers. It leaves such an unattractive, goopy mess. Perhaps that's why the wise guy Solomon said, "In many words there is emptiness" (Eccl. 5:7b NASB) and "Do not be hasty in word . . . let your words be few" (Eccl. 5:2 NASB).

Learning to be thrifty has always been a challenge for me. I'm a "more the merrier" kind of gal. Although, I have noticed, the more I ramble the more I gamble. There's such a thin line between having said just enough to having said way too much. Yet it is possible to say too much even in a few words. Like the time Les told our landlady her new muumuu (full-cut dress) looked like a refrigerator cover. Not good—trust me. We realized this when we were notified of a rent increase.

I guess this means we should be not only economical but also discriminating in our utterances.

Some verbal exchanges are harder to handle than others. Don't you hate it when you are given the wrong directions and waste precious time you can't afford looking for something that isn't there? I guess at one time or another we have all been misguided souls.

I remember when a doctor told me to stop eating fresh vegetables and fresh fruits. So I did. I faithfully followed his orders only to return a year later and have the same doctor tell me I should eat fresh veggies and fruit. When I challenged him, he said the medical profession had changed its theory for my type of digestive problem. The doctor didn't mean to misguide me, but according to new information, he had.

I know how that feels. I'm a mom. Need I say more? I've meant to do my mothering correctly, but at times I've been misguided. I remember early on someone telling me a baby should be allowed to cry out his discontent. Years later I was told babies only cry if they have a reason, and they need the assurance and the comfort of our touch. I guess every season brings a new wind of doctrine; it's easy to be blown off course.

Evidently that's what happened to Quacker B. Duck, who showed up at the Fox Briar Farm Inn in Paducah, Kentucky. A wind shear must have blown Quacker away from his flock because one day he dropped out of the sky smack-dab into the middle of the Fox Briar pond (and this was no tarp). After splashdown Quacker took a fancy to the Inn and the Clark family—he has never left. Actually, the misguided duck has eaten himself right into a case of fat feathers. The old boy can barely fly to the top of the fence post without flapping himself silly. Quacker couldn't get his chunky carcass back on course now if he wanted to.

Gratefully, if misguided, we humans can get back on course (no matter how chunky we've become). For he who designed the flight pattern of a bird has designated the steps of a woman. Scripture tells us to look for the "ancient path," and on this path the Lord is our flight instructor. He does not leave us to wander aimlessly alone or to feel hopelessly lost to the extent that we eventually quack up. Instead we are told to look up for our Redeemer draweth nigh.

Until Jesus returns we need to keep an eye on the sky—but not neglect to keep an eye on the road as well. For ducks are just one type of the many unexpected travelers we may encounter on the highways. Road signs throughout the land alert us to many different animal crossings. In Colorado they warn us of Horse Crossing, in Texas it's Donkey Crossing, in Iowa it's cows, in Michigan it's deer, in Maui it's turtles, and the list goes on. Why, my friends are even posting signs in their gardens for bunny, squirrel, and frog crossings. Evidently once Noah parked the ark the creatures aboard hotfooted it down the plank and scattered in all directions. Man followed in close pursuit and poured roadways right across Silver, Eeyore, Bossie, and Bambi's pathways. This has caused some startling results as man and beast continue to meet head-on.

I'm told my lumberjack father-in-law, Lawrence, met head-on with a nagging headache when a certain horse crossed his path. Seems he needed the service of an extra horse to help with the chores, so he rented a mare from a stable a few miles away from his logging camp. The horse's name was—what else—Silver.

Evidently Silver didn't like the rental agreement because every chance she got she ran home—nine long miles. Lawrence would retrieve Silver only to have her hightail it back to the stables at the first opportunity.

Finally, Lawrence, determined to secure Silver, locked her up in a small shack for safekeeping overnight. Early the next day, when Lawrence went to get Silver, the shack was gone. Yes, the shack and the horse were both gone. Actually, on close examination, Lawrence discovered that the shack hadn't actually vanished; it had just taken on a new form. Silver was apparently misnamed (she should have been dubbed Fury), for she had smashed the entire shed flatter than a flapjack. She then joyfully galloped the nine miles back to the safety of her stable humming "Don't Fence Me In" all the way. (She had probably watched too many old Gene Autrey movies.)

Silver had one thing on her mind—stall, sweet stall. Nothing and no one could redirect her energies until she had attained her goal.

Silver's determination—though not her method—gleams sterling. I personally am so often scattered in my goals that I end up stalled—and it's not a sweet experience. Perhaps I need blinders (with a silver lining) to keep me focused. Then I'd not only stay on the path, but I'd become more stable. Hi-ho, Silver!

My friend Gwen told me her grandfather had paid good silver for a team of workhorses. One day he was on his way to the beet fields when suddenly, a severe storm crossed his path. He knew he couldn't make it back to the farmstead without endangering his team, so he drove them quickly into a nearby vacant outbuilding. The building had a tin roof, and the storm had large hail. When the two collided, it frightened the team so badly that, instead of bolting (which would have been a normal reaction), the horses sat on their haunches. If they had bolted and run, they would have been clobbered to death because the hailstorm was so fierce that not a top was left on a beet. What was a leafy field one minute became a tossed salad of beet greens the next.

It fascinates me how a threatened animal will stop in its steps, like a freeze-frame, until the peril passes. Notice the next time you are near a rabbit, a squirrel, or a deer, how they will hold so still they often appear to be part of the landscape. Then, if they sense impending danger, they will scamper away.

We'd better take flight notes for our journey, for no doubt we will cross paths with threatening people and ominous storms. Next time you sense a storm brewing, be still, be ever so still. If you detect you are in danger, get out of harm's way. But don't be surprised if you are so stunned when the storm wallops you that you just plop down in a chair. Then, as your mind clears and you realize there appears to be no way of escape, try kneeling. Prayer has been known to provide a strong shelter in the midst of the storm.

It was a dark night after a storm when Bossie, a Holstein cow, wandered off her farm. She crossed one road after another and then meandered off the beaten path. At one point she lost her footing and fell spread-eagle to the ground. This is a dangerous and unnatural position for a cow (me, too!). Bellowing didn't help her pain, but it did help her owner, Gene, eventually to locate her. He brought in a winch and was finally able to get Bossie back on her feet. Gene was concerned that her struggle might have taken too much out of her, but Bossie lived—and thrived.

Lessons? (1) Discontentment can lead to wayward behavior, which sets us up for a fall. (2) Bellowing for help can be the first step necessary to restoration. (3) Struggles can help make us strong. Take heart. And oh, yes, for heaven's sake, don't be bossy.

Gene is a gentleman farmer and has been the "boss" of many animals over the years, although it's true that animals have minds of their own. He learned that early on. When he was only eight, he earned the money for his first cow, Daisy, by selling potatoes. Daisy was a Hereford and in time presented her proud owner with two calves.

Gene went on a camping trip once, and during his absence, Daisy roamed off. For a week she traipsed about the countryside. When Gene returned and finally found his cow, she had contracted pinkeye. Because it had not been attended to immediately, Daisy lost her sight. Young Gene was heartsick. He loved his cow, and he was afraid they would have to put her down.

But because Daisy had been around the barn a few times, so to speak, she still knew how to find her way between the pasture and her bed. Gene watched in amazement as Daisy would near the barn, then step gingerly forward until her horns would touch the building.

Then, pressing her horns lightly against the wood, she would trace her way around the barn to its opening and slip into her stall.

I love that story. No, not because I feel like an old cow, but because Daisy knew the path so well. I pray that I can follow in the Lord's footsteps so consistently that even when I can't "see," I'll continue to walk in his ways by faith. Why, even my old hard head, when bowed in his presence, can moo-ve me in the right direction. For when we graze in his pasture, we will rest in our beds—guaranteed.

Speaking of beds and rest, Les and I recently slept peacefully at the beautiful Fox Briar Inn. That is, once I identified the unusual evening lullaby breaking the stillness of the night—a herd of Belted Galloways (cows) in a nearby pasture. They were evidently saying good night to one another. You know the old "Good night, John Boy," "Good night, Momma," "Good night, Jason," "Good night, Mary Ellen" routine.

The next morning I stepped out my door onto the porch and saw the prettiest cows to ever cross my path. I didn't realize cows could be pretty, but these cattle looked like a herd of walking Oreo cookies. They had chocolate-black heads, front legs, bottoms, and back legs, with a belt of pure white around their centers. And they were amiable, like pets.

But their good looks didn't make them exempt from enemies. While we were there one calf died mysteriously, and two more disappeared. I was certain it was rustlers (flashbacks from my Gabby Hayes days), but the innkeeper, Ron, believed the culprits were coyotes. I preferred my solution—less gruesome, more intriguing, less final.

It's not unusual for me to prefer my solutions. I can actually become quite smitten with my own way of thinking. I love the mental aerobics of creative speculations—seeing how many possible answers I can conjure up for mysteries like the missing cows. For instance, the calves could have strayed off, but if you looked like an Oreo, would you stray far from your mother's milk? Nah, kids love milk and cookies.

The calves may have milked Mom for all she was worth, and she got fed up. (Or would that be dried up?) Perhaps Momma lost the joy of motherhood and sent the boys off to the brotherhood. Oh, utterly ridiculous—once a mom always a mom.

Maybe they were renegade calves kicking up their heels—they wanted to knock over a few pails. No, they would turn pale if their parents ever caught up with them and took off their belts to tan their hides.

Actually, I think the innkeeper was right—it was coyotes. Truth, like sour milk, is often hard to swallow. Yet I would rather face the whole truth than skim over reality with some two-percent rationalization.

I'm told there is nothing rational about a donkey and that a mule can be even more unreasonable when he crosses your path. Of course, there are exceptions to every rule. A man bragged joyfully about his jack mule. Why, he could yell down orders to Jack from the loft of the barn, and the mule below would acquiesce. Imagine that, a stubborn cuss walking in obedience to a voice command.

That should give us hope whether we are a Jack or a Jacqueline. For when we hear the voice of our Master and choose to walk in his ways, we are delivered from our deep-seated, resistant nature. I want to walk with such a willing and joyful heart that he never has to repeat himself. Unfortunately, I can be as stubborn as a ... well, you know. That's why I'm grateful Jesus not only crossed my path but also led me onto his. He knew I'd need help to find my way.

When my son Marty was a teenager, he found himself crossing the wrong path at the wrong time with the wrong animal. We lived at a youth camp, and Marty was involved in the chores. One day during animal feeding time he released the horses from the barn and strolled along behind as they trotted out to the field. Then, without warning, the horses turned and stampeded back toward the barn. All that stood between the sixteen horses and the barn was Marty, and he had no apparent way of escape. He stood transfixed as the horses' pounding hooves approached. A large quarter horse named Pepsi bore down upon Marty, but suddenly down-shifted and came to a screeching halt right in front of my son. This caused all the other horses to skirt around Pepsi, and so Marty was protected.

Whew, close calamity. We are grateful Pepsi crossed Marty's path. It was one of those times circumstances flew completely out of control. One of those times there wasn't a way of escape. One of those times there was no time to pray beyond, "Help!"

When the Lord sends unexpected (waddling, meandering, stampeding) messengers across our path, some may appear loony while others may nag, kick up their heels, or even turn on us. They are seldom whom we expect but often whom he chooses to use. And if he can use a mule, or a duck, or a cow, or a horse, then maybe, just maybe . . .

Fourteen

Unloading Zone

Marilyn Meberg

He who would travel happily must travel light.
—Antoine de Saint-Exupe'ry

Unloading Zone is a sign that offers deliciously absurd possibilities. What if each time we saw it we interpreted it literally? For instance, I am so frequently annoyed with the massive amount of "stuff" that seems to accumulate in my purse. Then that stuff reproduces into more stuff. In no time, I can't blow my nose, suck a cough drop, or move my car out of the garage because everything necessary to accomplish these tasks lies hidden in the depths of my purse.

Now, what if we assumed the Unloading sign were an invitation for us to dash to the curb and dump out our purses? Can't you just see the happy frenzy of activity? Perhaps the unloading persons would dump in the designated zone while another eager group would congregate in the loading section, eager to gather up the discarded items.

"You mean you don't want that emery board?"

"I'm dying to have that tin of peppermint Altoids; they claim to be curiously strong."

"Does anyone over there have gold paper clips?"

How about an Unloading Zone for car trunks? Let's see: rubber thongs from last summer, pamphlets from the Home Show promoting metal siding, two different sizes of bungee cord, a tire pump that doesn't, five huge cans of jalapeño cheese dip from the Price Club, a beach umbrella with a protruding spoke, and an eight-track tape disco version of the *Star Wars* theme song.

Of course, what could be *really* useful is an Unloading Zone for emotions. Perhaps this zone could be located on the outskirts of town, offering more privacy than a purse or trunk Unloading Zone. Some people would be stomping around, ranting and raving about the unfairness of life while another few would be sobbing, beating their chests, and periodically shouting, "Why?" We could possibly have "unloading encouragers" interspersed throughout the zone whose job it would be to say, "Good . . . that's good . . . you need to get that out . . . a little louder now . . . here, hit this pillow. Pretend it's your sewing teacher . . . That's right . . . good, very good."

You know, the more I think about this sign, the more I realize that life's journey is one of constant loading and unloading. It might be as benign as food, water, air, money, or cars. Or as startling as unloading a Smith-Wesson .38 caliber revolver. Let me unload that story for you.

Several months after Ken died, his wonderfully kind and engagingly red-necked cousin John insisted I needed a gun. "After all," he reasoned with me, "your house was already broken into once. Now that you're a widow, who knows what danger lurks beneath the kitchen window, behind the garage door, or down the street. You need to be able to protect yourself!"

As a child, I had determined to marry a rancher so that I could own horses, leap into the stored hay in the barn, fill my lungs with the heavenly scent of alfalfa, and shoot cans off a fence with my revolver. As I vaguely remembered this long-harbored desire, I didn't have the strength to resist John's logic. If I believed in the possibility of a person turning over in his grave, I can imagine Ken doing a major flip at the image of his wife brandishing a gun to ward off danger.

John insisted upon purchasing the gun for me, and then we went out target shooting. I hate to admit it, but I loved it. In fact, I was fairly good. I hit the bull's-eye three times with six shots. Neighborhood, look out!

At the conclusion of this satisfying triumph, John and Joanne, his happy shooting companion and wife, took me home, gave me instructions on gun cleaning, and then confidently drove away leaving me with a loaded Smith-Wesson revolver.

The more I thought of myself as a gun-totin' widow, the more uncomfortable I became. I couldn't imagine grabbing it and picking off intruders with one, maybe two shots. And what about my faith? Do I believe I have the moral right to shoot someone . . . even in my own home and in my own defense? I couldn't live, or for that matter die, with these thorny questions unanswered. And since I couldn't come to terms with it all, I hid my revolver under the bed in a leather pouch.

This was about the time I felt called to more closely monitor Luci's nefarious activities, which necessitated a move from Laguna Beach to her neck of the woods, in this case, Palm Desert.

So when my house in Laguna sold suddenly, I was thrilled with the sale. But I was thrown by the time line. The buyer wanted a one-month escrow. Two weeks out of that month I was traveling out of the state. When I returned from the second trip, I had only five days to pack and get out.

This was no small challenge, but I hummed right along until 3:00 A.M. two days before the movers were due to arrive. This is when I bolted out of bed with a startling realization. *I have a loaded gun under the bed, and I don't remember how to unload it! John lives two hours away. I can't ask him to come all the way down here, and besides, I don't want him to know I can't remember how to get the bullets out.*

It came to me the next morning. At times I am nothing short of brilliant after my second cup of morning tea. *Ah-ha! I have the answer to the dilemma that threw me out of bed last night. I'll simply take the gun down to the Laguna Beach police department and ask an officer to unload it. What an effortless solution!* I poured my third cup of tea.

Even so, this plan was not without its challenges. What if I were stopped by a police officer on the way to the station and he found my loaded gun in the car? How on earth would I explain that major infraction of the law? Would he or she buy my explanation that, yes, I knew I had a loaded gun, but I was actually at that very moment on my way downtown to the police station to have it unloaded? Mercy!

I decided to put the Smith-Wesson in my winter white Anne Klein purse (that should look fairly innocent) and carefully place it behind the spare tire in the trunk. I was a bit troubled as to which way the gun should be pointed: at me, persons to the left of the car, individuals to the right of the car, or straight at whomever was following me. No one could see it, of course, but what if it discharged? I had heard some pretty horrific stories about that sort of thing. I opted for those to the left of the car . . . no reason.

Leaving my potentially lethal purse in the trunk, I strolled into the police station with a look of studied casualness. A couple of policemen stood in a corner chatting and several disreputable looking young men slouched in some straight-back chairs. I stood at the counter for a moment, but no one even glanced my way. I drummed my nails, cleared my throat, and then loudly dropped my keys. Still nothing. After about five minutes I said to nobody in particular, "Excuse me, but I have a loaded gun and—" A number of blue uniforms immediately surrounded me; no one looked friendly.

I tried to explain my situation while they scowled at me from their tight blue circle. "My husband died six years ago, you see . . . his cousin thought I should have a gun . . . I was robbed once, you know . . . you came up and searched for fingerprints. Anyway, I'm moving . . . the gun's loaded . . . I need to get the bullets out of it before the movers take my bed apart . . . right now it's in my winter white purse in the trunk of my car. I'm parked in front of my veterinarian's office right across the street . . . Can you help me?"

Eyebrows raised, then they glanced woodenly at each other, nodded, and moved en masse out of the station to my car.

Desperate to lighten the atmosphere I said, "I guess I should have parked in an Unloading Zone." No response.

When I opened the trunk, one of the uniforms said, "Where's the weapon, ma'am?" I thought of Jack Webb on *Dragnet*.

"Behind the spare tire, sir."

"Spare tire?"

"Yes, sir . . . in the winter white purse."

"Winter white purse?"

"Yes, sir. Would you like me to unzip it?"

The trunk, spare tire, and winter white purse were immediately blocked from my view by a blue uniform. I heard a sound that indicated the removal of bullets, and then the blue blur turned around, handed me my purse, and asked how I wanted to deal with "the weapon."

I asked how much it would sell for. They quoted a nice figure, enough to buy a few lunches, so I returned the gun to my purse. They kept the bullets.

The next day the movers dismantled my bed, and I moved to Palm Desert.

Now, you may be worried about this gun business. You're thinking things like, "Marilyn, how on earth can you trivialize the seriousness of the damage guns do in our society? The very idea of owning a gun or using a gun is abhorrent! But it's even worse to sell it; who knows what sort of creep might buy it? What about your Christian witness? You certainly aren't setting a good example."

You know what? I'm muttering right along with you. I can't justify owning or using a gun. And yet, I have some dear Christian friends who can't imagine not owning a gun for responsible use and protection. These people feel deeply about our right to protect ourselves with firearms should it be necessary. Nothing in me rises up in judgment of them. But I personally have decided that I will not contribute my gun to what's already "out there." So my gun is still with me, still in my winter white purse, carefully hidden away. But this time it's unloaded and not under the bed. Obviously, unloading isn't always as easy as one may think at first.

Another dangerous item that could use its own, carefully monitored Unloading Zone is anger. Because it can be so toxic, it should not even be in the city limits. This zone becomes then much more specific than the broad-based zone for unloading generic emotion on the outskirts of town. To maintain at least a degree of civility and order, it might be wise to post a few policies for those who come to unload. Perhaps a few policy enforcers could mingle throughout the crowd; you would recognize them by their bright red shirts. A few policies that come to mind for this zone are:

1. All unloaders must remain fully clothed.
2. Screamers may have unlimited access to the water fountains. (Spitters will be fined heavily.)
3. Unloaders who are angry but not sure why will be provided with "pondering stools" at the very edge of the zone.
4. Rubber barrel kickers will be directed to a special location in the zone (next to the rubber bat swingers).
5. Those who wish to write letters spewing forth venom and ire will be provided with yellow legal pads and extra thick pencils. The writers will be seated next to burning

incinerators to destroy the written venom and ire once the exercise has served its purpose. No mailboxes will be allowed in the zone, and the writers, prior to leaving, will submit to a full body search by the red-shirted policy enforcers.

6. Those who wish to read their letters of venom and ire to their intended recipients will be instructed by the policy enforcers to imagine their recipients sitting in a chair listening to the venom and ire. (Chairs, paper, pencils, and tissues will be provided through the generosity of a corporate grant.)

7. No one carrying a winter white purse will be allowed in the zone.

8. No one may vomit on another. (More about this later.)

9. Unloaders may stay in the zone no longer than forty-five minutes. If they insist on staying beyond this time, they will be bussed to the self-pitying zone in the heart of town.

10. The zone closes at sunset.

While it's fun to deal playfully with the subject of unloading anger, it does a disservice to one of the most volatile and misunderstood emotions we as human beings experience. So, if you don't mind, I'd like to camp on this subject a little longer and with a little more seriousness.

As you know, God created us with a broad spectrum of emotional potential. On one end of the spectrum, we experience giggles, gladness, and joy; on the other end, sadness, disappointment, and anger. It is important that we feel all of these emotions, and even express them, but by the same token, we must learn to express them in nontoxic and appropriate ways.

Many Christians believe anger is an ungodly and unsanctified emotion and must never even be felt, much less expressed. Yet Paul said in Ephesians 4:26, "Be ye angry and sin not" (KJV). We do not sin when we feel anger; we sin when we express it inappropriately.

Jesus felt and expressed anger a number of times, which are described in Scripture. In Mark 3, Jesus got angry at the Pharisees when they attempted to arrest him for healing a man with a withered hand on the Sabbath. To them, he had broken the Sabbath law by doing work. Scripture says Jesus looked at them in anger—anger at their legalistic adherence to a law that ignored human need.

In the familiar scene described in Matthew 21:12 Jesus grabbed whips and drove the money changers stumbling and scrambling out of the temple because they were price gouging the animal sacrifices used for the ritual of confession of sin. He was infuriated with their behavior and accused them of turning a place of worship into a den of thieves.

Jesus called the Pharisees "blind fools," "whitewashed tombs," "murderers," "serpents," and "miserable frauds." He was anything but passive when it came to human and spiritual injustice. He was angry, and he expressed it.

Anger can be a form of positive energy. It can cause us to rise up and take a necessary stand against an action, practice, or law that must be changed. We can't passively stand by in the midst of society's wrongs.

If expressed appropriately, anger can be beneficial in our personal relationships as well. If we feel violated in any way by someone, we can feel free to express our anger to that person rather than deny or bottle up our feelings.

But now we get to the tricky part. Most of us are peacekeepers; we don't want to confront, even in a kind and sane way. It's too frightening. What if the person won't listen, what if our feelings are ridiculed, what if she refuses to "own" her part? What if he accuses and hurts us even more?

Rather than risk all that, we become the keepers of "holy grudges." (I call them holy grudges because we reverence and pay homage to them.) This then places anger in a new category. It's no longer a potential instrument for positive change. In the Living Bible, Ephesians 4:26 reads, "If you are angry, don't sin by nursing your grudge." Once again we see that the emotion of anger is not the sin, but we can sin in what we do with it. It is our responsibility to at least try to communicate our anger, but it is not our responsibility if the other person fails to respond.

The next step is to forgive the other person, even if it would seem to us that the person doesn't deserve our forgiveness. To forgive is to lay down our holy grudge and walk away from it. (Maybe we should have an Unloading Zone for holy grudge holders. But that's probably a poor use of land since most grudge holders refuse to unload . . . forget it.)

However, the bad news is that it's humanly impossible to forgive someone who has wronged us. To truly forgive and forget is contrary to our nature. But there's good news. Through the Spirit of God, it is possible to forgive those who betray, abandon, cheat, lie about, scorn, and/or reject us. Forgiving is so antithetical to our natural way that if we don't release our grudges to him and pray sincerely for his love and forgiveness to flow through us, it will never happen. The act of forgiveness is a God-inspired and God-produced accomplishment. To attempt that act in our own strength is to expect failure.

Forgiveness is not a Marilyn thing, but a God thing. I find that realization comforting and freeing.

At this point, I feel compelled to further develop rule number nine for anger unloaders. This is the one that reads, "No one may vomit on another." I realize that this rule may seem ridiculous and far-fetched. No one in his right mind purposely vomits all over another person. Well, my fourteen-month-old grandson sometimes . . . Perhaps we should change the rule to read, "No one over the age of two . . ."

Anyway, this kind of behavior is simply not tolerated in a cultured society. So, what if we were to meet for lunch next Thursday, and contrary to social custom, I proceeded to "bluck" up all over your plaid dress, saying something like, "Wow. I feel so much better"?

You might respond, "Wh–what on earth was that about? Why didn't you go do that in private?!"

Interestingly enough, we often do the "bluck" thing with our anger. Sometimes we not only bluck on family and friends but also on perfect strangers. We dispense our anger on salespersons, airline personnel, receptionists, plumbers, doctors, and dentists. (Actually, dentists deserve it. What can they expect when they cram everything in your mouth but their hydraulic stool?) But spewing anger is every bit as unacceptable as vomiting tomato soup. Perhaps the next time you think of blucking, you could pause, swallow hard, and consider a more appropriate and less, shall we say, "vivid" way to deal with your anger.

We can quickly lacerate another's soul by unloading violent anger. I call it the "verbal terminator" response, and we can use it to truly hurt others.

That's assuming you're good at it, which my son, Jeff, wasn't as he was growing up. When he was four years old, he and his little girlfriend Nell were playing in the sandbox. Nell wasn't exhibiting democratic behavior, and so after she had snatched Jeff's very last Tonka truck and put it in her "sand garage," Jeff stood up, his little face red with indignation. "You're a big, fat burp!" he exploded. Nell seemed flattered and continued in her undemocratic ways. I thought, *With maturity and time, Jeff will undoubtedly hone his verbal skills into more effective terminating.*

You are undoubtedly aware of James 3:8, which reads, "But no one can tame the tongue; it is a restless evil and full of deadly poison" (NASB). I hate recognizing the truth of that verse. How quickly and effortlessly I resort to the use of my untamed tongue to put someone in her "place."

To further cramp my style and thwart my verbal skills, there's Proverbs 15:1–2: "A gentle answer turns away wrath, but a harsh word stirs up anger. The tongue of the wise makes knowledge acceptable, but the mouth of fools spouts folly" (NASB). In spite of our (how do you like the way I drew you into my guilt camp?) frequent failings to live out this truth, the formula for verbalizing anger is so clear in verse two: "The tongue of the wise makes knowledge acceptable."

If I am wise and can maintain my dignity as well as preserve the dignity of the other person, I can possibly communicate my grievances in a way that is acceptable. That is what effective communication is: two people hearing each other without uncontrolled tonguing. So often though, we become impatient with the process and simply finish off the exchange with a few choice words, phrases, or sentences, then huff off leaving the other bleeding and wounded.

Proverbs 15:4 reads, "A soothing tongue is a tree of life" (NASB). You know, you and I aren't the only ones (notice how I continue to enlist you in my camp?) who struggle with a tongue that is anything but soothing. I find great comfort, as well as a giggle, in Psalm 39:1–3, in which David describes his efforts at taming his tongue. He says: "I will guard my ways, that I may not sin with my tongue; I will guard my mouth as with a muzzle" (NASB).

Don't you love that? A custom-fit muzzle. The problem is, David didn't have a muzzle. Instead he continued to stew over the prosperity of the wicked. He describes his grief as being stirred and his heart as burning. Then the "fire blazed up," and his tongue burst into speech. We can only hope David was in the anger Unloading Zone when his tongue burst.

Talk about an unloader; David unloaded throughout the psalms. One reason I so love his God-inspired writing is that he didn't hold or hide his emotions. I find the psalms therapeutic because whatever I may be feeling, I can find a psalm in which David expresses the same feeling.

Not only am I encouraged by David's empathy and personal identification, but he also teaches me by example where I need to

unload as I journey through life. I need to unload with God . . .
sometimes even *on* God.

David had a candid relationship with God. He told God exactly
how he felt all the time, holding nothing back. This kind of vulnerability reflects David's tremendous security in God's constancy.

Sometimes I think that unloading on God might be disre-
spectful, signify a lack of faith, or be inappropriate for a Christian.
But that kind of thinking keeps me from true intimacy with him.
In reality, it means I don't trust him, that if he really heard my soul,
he would disapprove and maybe leave, so I better be sure to always
put on my best face.

God doesn't leave (he promised), and he already really knows
me. That's a bit mind-boggling, isn't it? If I can truly believe it,
then I can fully trust him. And if I fully trust him, like David, I can
unload on him. Psalm 51:6 reads, "You [God] deserve honesty from
the heart; yes, utter sincerity and truthfulness" (TLB).

I have to admit, more often than not I "put on a face" with
God. To express my occasional disappointment, my periodic lack
of faith, or my frequent lack of comprehension seems too rude. But
if I don't approach him honestly, I suffer the consequences of a surface relationship with the very One who not only invites my truthfulness but also is the One fully able to hear it. Maybe that's why
I'm so inspired by David's "unloading philosophy" expressed in
Psalm 55:16–18. "As for me, I shall call upon God, and the LORD
will save me. Evening and morning and at noon, I will complain
and murmur, and He will hear my voice" (NASB).

Can you imagine unloading on God morning, noon, and night,
murmuring and complaining, and still be confident that "He shall
hear my voice"? Now there's a security I'd like to load up on! In fact,
I think I will. In so doing, I just might be seen less in the other
Unloading Zones, except, of course, for the purse and trunk ones.

Fifteen

Children at Play

Barbara Johnson

Second to the right, and straight on till morning.
—J. M. BARRIE, *PETER PAN*

T he sign Children at Play announces that something
joyous is happening in this world that is often defined
by survival and acquiring money and sustenance. We are graced
to know that children are still hard at work just playing.

I remember when I was a child in wintry Michigan. One day
occurs to me, not because it was anything special, but because it
was so typical of my childhood. We had dressed warmly, gathered
our sleds, and stepped out into a magical white world. Bright
nuggets of ice had fallen from the branches of trees and sparkled
like transient diamonds along the path. The soft swish of our feet
as we walked through the snow was the only sound besides the tin-
kle of ice-clad branches, as a slight breeze nudged them against
each other. Out of sheer exuberance, we fell back into the soft
snow and windmilled our arms to make angels. The trick was to
stand up without ruining the angel.

Bundling up in fuzzy snowsuits and black rubber galoshes with metal clasps down the front seemed a small price to pay for all the fun of playing Fox and Geese. We would stamp a big circle into the snow, an X crisscrossing it, and then chase one another, careful not to step outside the paths. Afterward we came inside to drape wet mittens and hats over hot-air radiators and to drink hot cocoa.

The next day, we would put on all the clothes again and take a "Silver Streak" sled down a nearby hill. Or we might use a round metal tray or a cardboard box for a really exciting experience.

We had lots of snow in Michigan. I think of the flakes falling pure and white and my gathering chunks of it to make bowls of snow ice cream. I added nuts, raisins, and sugar and ate it quickly before it melted. Icicles were fun, too. We made a game of sucking them into sharp points. Even now, remembering, I feel like a child again.

These types of memories never fade completely. Neither does the one in which I stuck my tongue on a metal railing and it froze there. I also remember the chapped hands and frostbitten feet that would turn white and painful. But the pain associated with living in that climate is far removed from the memories of childhood fun.

That's like life. We endure the painful times, but later, when we reflect back, the pain has sort of drained away, and the memories are bittersweet.

Recounting other children's antics helps us to relive our childhoods and to enjoy the humor that bubbles up out of the mouths of children. These stories remind us that we can still capture that playful spirit they so easily exude.

I remember the one that appeared in *Reader's Digest* some months ago. A four-year-old girl and three-year-old boy walked hand in hand to a neighbor's house. The girl had to stretch to reach the doorbell, and when the neighbor appeared, the little girl announced, "We're playing house. This is my husband, and I am his wife. May we come in?"

Amused by the scene, the woman played along. "By all means," she said, and offered them some lemonade and cookies.

When a second glass of lemonade was offered, the little girl said, "No, thank you. We have to go now. My husband wet his pants."

Then there was the kindergartner who was miffed when her mother couldn't recall the song "Baby Pockets." "The teacher said you would know it," she insisted and then proved the teacher right by belting out, "Bay-bee, Bay-bee Pockets, king of the wild frontier!"

I heard about a little girl whose brother wasn't attending school. When the teacher asked her why, she answered, "My brother can't breathe good because he has sixty-five roses." This puzzled the teacher until she learned that the brother had Cystic Fibrosis.

Of course, kids get things mixed up sometimes, like the one who called Noah's wife Joan of Ark. Or the one who said the fourth commandment is to humor thy father and mother. Another said that Lot's wife was a pillar of salt by day and a ball of fire at night. Christians have only one spouse, a boy said; this is called monotony. Another said the Pope lives in the Vacuum. One little girl came home from school and announced, "The school nurse looked through everybody's hair to make sure we don't have any headlights."

While we can learn from children, the reverse obviously takes place, but not always in the way we intend. Our children are watching us live, and what we are shouts louder than anything we say. When we encircle them with love, they will be loving. When we meet life with laughter and a twinkle in our eye, they will develop a sense of humor. Don't just stand there pointing your finger to the heights you want your children to scale. Start climbing, and they will follow. Start playing!

No matter what your early childhood was like—the best of all growing up experiences or the worst—you and only you are in charge of your life now. Your current thinking shapes your future and can create a life of unlimited joy, if you approach it joyfully.

A mother of two small children learned that one day. She had become absorbed in her reading while her three-year-old daughter and five-month-old son played quietly nearby. The son loved his older sister, who had adored him since his birth.

Suddenly the mother realized the children were no longer playing in the room. Panic-stricken, she went looking for them. She found them playing happily in her daughter's bedroom. Relieved and yet upset, she reminded her daughter, "You know you are not allowed to carry your little brother! He is too little, and you could hurt him if you dropped him or he fell."

She answered, "I didn't, Mommy."

"Well, how did he get here all the way from the family room?" the mother asked suspiciously.

"I rolled him," the little girl said with a smile. Can you imagine how this kid felt on his journey down the hall?

For many years when our kids were growing up, we lived next door to a darling older woman who lived alone and who had never had children. But she enjoyed our kids and was like a next-door grandmother to them.

We had a swimming pool in our backyard, and it was always full of children shrieking and jumping and slipping down the slide. A huge inner tube from a tractor occupied a large section of the pool. The kids would jump from it, and the noise was often deafening.

I was forever asking them to tone it down and stop yelling because I was afraid the noise would disturb our neighbor. One day when I was apologizing to her for the noise, she said, "Oh, Barbara, I love to hear the children laughing and playing. They are such happy sounds. I leave my window open so I can hear the joyful noises." Laughing, joyful sounds? They always sounded raucous to me. Guess I needed to learn a new perspective and to lighten up a little.

Laughter is the key to surviving the special stresses of the child-rearing years. I believe if you can see the delightful side of your assignment, you can also deal with the difficult. Laughter helps, regardless of your situation.

Need help bringing laughter to life? Well, how long has it been since you played the way children do? Simple things like eating watermelon on top of the water tower at night, jumping into piles of autumn leaves, or gathering big armfuls of lilacs and taking them to friends' homes so they will smell like spring. The value of fun lies in the spirit of it.

No matter your age, it's possible to become a child again. You are never too old to recover your childhood.

Look for ways to enjoy your day, however small or trivial. Even finding a convenient parking space can bring you joy. Look for fun. Just sitting on a bench and watching people gives us joy in a childlike way.

If snow falls where you live, make snowballs, put them in the freezer, and give them to the kids next July. They will love it, and it will provide you with a happy memory of the previous winter. It's one more way to join in the playful world of children.

Have you ever watched a child swat madly at specks of dust that hang suspended in a shaft of sunlight? Children delight in such innocent, simple things.

If it takes climbing windmills, marching in a parade, or ascending the down escalator to break out of your little, proper, plastic, grown-up mold, do it. Become a real dingy person—not din-gee but ding-ee. Even if people think you are fresh out of the rubber room.

Learn to find fun in unlikely places. Fun is a mystery that can't be trapped like an animal or caught like the flu. It comes without bidding if you have eyes to see it.

Recently the mailman left me a lumpy manila envelope. Its contents puzzled me until I read the accompanying letter from a special friend. "This is a Love Kit," she explained, "and each enclosed item represents a promise that God made about blessing your life. I'm sending it to remind you how much he cares about you, and how much I do, too."

A Scripture verse was attached to each item in the package, and so I pulled out my Bible and, one by one, looked up the verses:

A bar of candy: Psalm 34:10
A shiny dime: Philippians 4:19
A key chain: Proverbs 3:33
A packet of colorful tissues: Job 11:16
A big red eraser: Jeremiah 31:34
A Band-Aid: Psalm 147:3
A pretty comb: Matthew 10:30–31

By the time I had finished reading about God's abundant provision for my needs, comfort, forgiveness, healing, and protection, I was wearing a wide smile. The ordinary but whimsical trinkets had brightened my day, and browsing through the Bible had refreshed my mood. I continued to look up Scriptures so that I could send another friend a Love Kit. Seems childlike? Maybe so.

The Love Kit reminded me that God loves those who don't know how to be anyone but themselves. This is one reason he made children, and that's why he leaves a little child in each of us.

We need to let that little child out once in a while, and a good place to do it is with our kids. Did you know that the most efficient water power in the world is a child's tears? Well, I think it's time to fight back! For far too long parents have driven themselves to despair trying to get along with their teenagers. I suggest it's time for us to drive *them* crazy. Here are a few suggestions:

Insist on putting a picture of yourself on his wall.

Get a mother-daughter outfit and follow her around wherever she goes.

Deduct withholding tax from his allowance.

Take her mirror away so she can't practice smiling.

Hang around when his friends come over.

Reset all the push buttons on the car radio to all your favorite
stations.

Make the telephone cord one foot shorter than the distance
to her bed.

Iron his jeans.

Set her scale five pounds too heavy.

Invite his teacher to dinner.

I love children and the way they are able to be so open and
honest with us. They don't ask us to change; they love us as we
are. Kids aren't touchy like adults, who easily get their feelings
hurt. And they are believers—they accept what we say at face
value.

We adults raise hard questions that we want answered before
we will commit ourselves to Jesus. But a child accepts the truth as it
is told to him and shows an avid curiosity to learn more. Jesus invites
us to come to him as a little child, trusting, unafraid, and curious,
simply believing that he will forgive us and save us from the consequences of our wrongdoing. Ask Jesus to humble you and instill in
you a childlike faith.

The other day I was in a Christian bookstore wandering
through the children's section. I watched a little girl as she picked
up a stuffed toy lamb. "This is how Jesus carries the lamb," she told
her mother. She then demonstrated by lovingly cradling the stuffed
animal in her arms. "Sometimes he carries the lamb like this," she
continued in a sweet, instructive voice. She carefully placed the
lamb over her shoulder as if it were the most precious creature that
ever existed.

Her mother listened politely, but I became teary-eyed. The
girl's "lesson" spoke of her confidence in a loving Savior who

treasured her. I felt uplifted the rest of the day as I remembered her sweet spirit and her message.

We may not be able to physically go back and make a new start, but we can start from now and make a brand new end. We can begin today to join children at play and to choose to see the world afresh, even when hard things are happening.

Once a reporter stood in front of a fire as it consumed a house and then turned to see the homeowners and their little son watching it burn. The reporter, fishing for a human interest angle, said to the boy, "Son, it looks as if you don't have a home anymore." The little boy promptly answered, "Oh, yes, we have a home. We just don't have a *house* to put it in."

Children also teach us new levels of compassion. A young mother told me about her dismay when her little girl came home late from school one day. When she asked her daughter why she was so late, the little girl explained that her friend had dropped a china doll on the sidewalk, and it had broken into pieces. "So you stopped to help her fix the doll?" the mother asked.

"No, Mommy. We knew we couldn't fix it, but I stopped to help her cry."

Somehow children understand compassion without ever having it explained to them, which reminds us adults that maybe we could work on this area in our own lives.

Children have a lot to offer us. They don't have agendas, but they do have hope and a simple view of life. They are quick to trust and slow to dislike others. They play easily by themselves or with other kids. We need to imitate them, becoming childlike without being childish. It's easy to lose sight of the joy that a simple approach to others can bring, but if we close our eyes and wish really hard, we just might recall a tinge of what it's like to experience life as a child.

Sixteen

School Zone

Patsy Clairmont

We've come a distance, but we still have a distance to go.
— TRADITIONAL

School Zone. Slow down; watch out for the kiddies. In fact, why don't you pull into the school lot and park for awhile? I'd like you to take a journey back to your days as a student. Remember early September? In the Midwest the leaves are still on the trees, but some have begun to tinge with autumn's glitter. The nip in the morning air enhances the thrill of a fresh beginning. You start off for school wearing a sweater only to shed it by noon and then lug it home with books and homework by day's end.

The first day of school was always a mix of anticipation and intimidation for me. I couldn't wait to see my friends, meet new ones, evaluate my teachers, find my locker, and of course, check out the boys. But I was also intimidated at the thought of meeting new friends, being evaluated by my teachers, finding my locker, and of course, being checked out by the boys.

A highlight of each year for me was that moment when I got to pick out new school supplies. Something about a spanking new, blue, loose-leaf notebook filled with crisp lined paper and colored tabs boasting semester classes filled me with the expectation that this could be my best academic year yet. I could choose from an array of writing choices in my pencil case including a marking pencil that was red on one end and blue on the other—one of my favorites. (Remember when our parents used a knife to scrape off a place on the pencils for our names?)

The eraser was my most used item and least appreciated. As I erased I often scrubbed a hole through the paper and left dark smudges all over my faulty efforts. Then there was the compass, which I used maybe once throughout my formal education. Yet I always bought a new one at the onset of the school year. You remember them, don't you? Those sharp metal tools used for measuring angles, drawing circles, or carving initials in desks? I have no idea where my old compasses disappeared to at the end of each school season, but one thing I know for sure—I didn't wear them out.

What did wear out, though, was my interest in school. Somewhere along my school journey I took a radical turn. School days changed into cruel daze as I lost interest and motivation. In high school instead of math I was into makeup, reports turned into retorts, I exchanged social studies for social events, and suddenly the Jims in school looked more interesting than the gym. My pursuit of boyfriends became far more important than my bookwork.

Then, as a lark, I ran away from home with a friend who had been harshly disciplined by her parents. School had become such an emotional hardship that I was open to any form of escape. Running sounded like more of an adventure than sitting in school, and besides, I was a risk taker. Little did I realize the concern I would cause my family . . . or the lessons I would learn.

I thought my newfound freedom from school and home rules would feel liberating. Wrong. I was scared, lonely, and unprepared to face the rigors of real life, which included picking potatoes for pocket change. It was hard work—harder than homework and even more boring. Do you know how similar potatoes are? Oh, sure the eyes are in different places, but after one stint in the fields, I never wanted to see another bespectacled spud.

The idea that I could spend my life as "Patsy the Potato Picker," knee-deep in dirt with a wrenched back, was not appealing. My friend and I returned to our homes after two weeks, and a few months later I dropped out of high school and enrolled in a new school—Marriage U. I was seventeen. I had wanted to marry Les when I was sixteen, but I couldn't talk him into it. I believed marriage would answer all my problems and make me happy. But instead of wedded bliss, I felt as if I were simply now attending a different school—one I wasn't prepared for.

I soon became emotionally troubled—and troubling. I was unreasonable, demanding, suspicious, and controlling. I began to suffer anxiety attacks and became an agoraphobic (a condition of abnormal fears). I spent years roaming in circles, trying to find my way out of my emotional labyrinth. The good news is that during that desperate time I started to ask questions instead of proclaim answers. I began to search for truth instead of shout edicts. When that happened, without my realizing it, God reopened my school records and decided it was time for me to resume my education.

I didn't go back to public school, but I began to read. I read everything I could get my hands on that offered insight and hope. I even opened a small Christian bookstore in my home to supply people in the community with books and also to meet my own growing appetite for knowledge. I read truckloads of books—good books, some even great. I developed an insatiable hunger for insight. And as I applied the insights, I advanced in my educational process.

When I ventured from my home (and out of my agoraphobia) I attended a group called Recovery—a self-help program for those suffering with anxiety. I was nervous about it, though, and convinced Les to wait outside in the parking lot during the meetings in case I panicked and needed to ditch class. But what I found inside were others who felt and struggled in the same ways as I did. What a relief and what a learning experience. Just knowing I was not alone released me from a lot of guilt, confusion, and inner stress. Although there was one meeting . . .

I was walking toward the church where the Recovery group met, and as I passed by a convenience store, I spotted a runaway car rolling along on its merry way. The owner had entered the store when his empty vehicle decided to make a break for it. The car was moving backward toward a busy highway. I started to yell and sprint at the same time. The driver didn't hear my cries, and so I caught up with his car, opened the door, jumped in, and hit the brake. The runaway and I stopped just three feet from the oncoming traffic.

The owner came out of the store then and saw me waving at him like a frantic cheerleader. He strolled to his car and nonchalantly took over the wheel.

I entered the meeting, my heart pounding like a set of bongo drums thumping out Bobalou. I sat down just as the group leader asked, "Can anyone give us an example of feeling stressed?" Talk about a visual aid—I was my own show-and-tell!

Remember show-and-tell? I liked to bring things to school to show off. I just didn't want to get up in front of everyone and talk. Now that was stress. Throughout my elementary and high school years I'd rather hide in my desk than make an up-front appearance. I'd take a failing mark before I'd risk the visual scrutiny of my classmates. (Even though outside of school I loved making scenes.)

Then, for some strange reason, I took a speech class in my sophomore year. What made the class truly intimidating were the juniors and seniors.

The last assignment of the year was to write a report and present it to our classmates in the auditorium. At first I wasn't even going to try, but then an idea for a speech popped into my head and wouldn't leave. I planned to talk about the teen's world, using the acrostic, *teenager*.

I worked on this project for weeks, which was unheard of for me. I probably put more effort into that assignment than any I had ever done. I can still remember how scared yet excited I was on the day of the presentation. The walk onto and across the stage felt like a cross-country trek. My legs were weak and my mouth was dry, but I delivered my speech. A real sense of accomplishment surged through me as I made my way back to my seat.

The teacher gave me a *B*, which for me was a high grade, but my speech had gone so well I couldn't help wondering why I hadn't received an *A*. So I asked and then I wished I hadn't.

The teacher told me flat out he didn't believe it was *my* speech. My poor grades in other classes reinforced his suspicions. But since he couldn't prove it, he had given me the *B*.

His words covered me in shame. I was devastated. I was humiliated. I was defeated.

I've always wondered what might have been if my speech teacher had perceived my rare moment of success as an indicator of potential rather than something suspicious. He might have made a tremendous contribution to the life of a floundering young student. Instead, I felt such embarrassment I didn't attempt to write or speak publicly for years.

Of course, my teacher had good reason for suspicion as I was a below-average student. I didn't turn in most of my assignments, and I sometimes fell asleep in my classes—the school zone would become the snooze zone. I was a late-night girl. I wasn't allowed to go out on school nights, but I did have a telephone in my bedroom. A baby blue phone. A princess phone . . . with a lighted dial. Instead of studying or sleeping, I was chatting. Big time. My friend Carol and I would gossip, giggle, and commiserate for hours on end—mostly about boys, clothes, and music. After her parents had gone to bed, Carol would sneak out to the family phone in the kitchen to call me. I would slip down between the sheets with the phone, and we would talk into the wee hours. Sometimes we would even fall asleep while on the phone . . . me in my canopy bed and poor Carol huddled in a heap on the floor. Z-z-z. The next day dawned far too early for two girls whose eyes were on tilt and whose brains were in siesta land.

The Lord is a long-suffering teacher even when his students fall asleep. Remember Gethsemane? Z-z-z. Actually, he was the first teacher with enough patience to work with me. He has a myriad of ways to accomplish his good work and higher education within us. As I grew into adulthood, the Lord used my emotional desperation to motivate me toward change. I never imagined during those emotionally unsteady years, as I consumed libraries of information and attended scads of classes and lectures, that the Lord was supplementing my limited schooling. I just knew I needed h-e-l-p if I were to survive. That help came through study, instruction, experience, and a plethora of teachers. And school is still in session.

Of course, I continue to love recess. Wheee! I have learned along the journey how important play is to our lives as long as it is our minor and not our major. We were designed to work and to work heartily. I don't think there is any sweeter sleep than that which follows a diligent day's work. But without respite, work will wear us to a frazzle. Recess keeps the dazzle in our footwork.

Speaking of dazzling feet, I can't think about school without recalling the pair of red Dorothy shoes I had one year. They had a stylish heel, could be seen for miles in all directions, and my friends admired them almost as much as I did. But I couldn't click them together and be transported to school. I had to travel in the same mundane manner as everyone else—on a bus.

Our lackluster bus driver never smiled or spoke except to give a reprimand. And he did that with rigor. If his goal was to intimidate us into proper behavior, he was a smashing success. He did not tolerate yelling, cursing, or tardiness. And once his bus started moving, he stopped for no one. He seemed to actually enjoy driving past those students who were late, leaving them to hoof their way to school.

This bus driver represented a challenge. I decided he must be lonely, sad, or friendless. I wanted to win him over. And so, every day I would smile and say, "Good morning," and when he would drop us off, I would always say, "Good-bye." He never answered, and he never smiled. A couple of times I thought I saw his head nod as if acknowledging me, but I wasn't certain. Then it happened.

I was late because I had slept in. (Who me? Yawn.) I knew I would be in trouble with my mom and the school if I didn't get on that bus. I sped out the door and down the street, clutching my books and purse. But just as I ran down the last block toward the bus, the big yellow vehicle closed its doors and pulled out onto the highway. My heart sank. Even with fancy footwork, I hadn't made it in time. I stopped dead in my tracks as the bus prepared to pass me by. Then suddenly the giant vehicle's brakes hissed and screeched, and the bus groaned to a halt. Four lanes of traffic came to a stop as the lights flashed, and the doors popped open. Startled, I hesitated, then I bolted toward the doors, leaped up the steps, and dashed to a seat. There was an astonished hush on board as the doors cranked closed and we resumed our travels. I looked up into the rearview mirror and saw a twinkle in the bus driver's eyes. When I deboarded, I thanked him. But he never said a word. He didn't have to. Stopping the bus for me was the biggest smile he could have ever given me.

I felt as if I had made a friend (more like a silent partner) in the bus driver. And I have learned that friends are important in gaining a solid education. In fact, friends frequently are like a ruler the Lord uses to nudge me so I will sit up taller and stop speaking out of turn.

Barbara, Luci, and Marilyn are great nudgers. They allow me to bounce thoughts off them without making me feel like a dunce, and then they help me measure my words. They also are women of definite ideas as well as examples of compassionate communicators. Tricky balance. They measure out heart-kindness and don't allow their tongues to rule or ruin their relationships with others.

Les had the joy of learning lessons in a one-room schoolhouse in the Upper Peninsula of Michigan. Thirty-two students representing eight grades filled the room. A student would begin in the first grade on the front row of seats and each year move up a grade and back a row until by graduation he was in the last row. Three students were in my husband's eighth-grade graduating class—two girls and Les. He held the enviable position in his final year of sitting in the desk right next to the door.

That meant Les could be the last one in the room every day and the first one out. His desire to be out the door grew when he entered high school, and in the eleventh grade, Les quit. He, too, returned as an adult and took care of unfinished school business.

Les and I had to grow up to realize the importance of a formal education. But we have also come to appreciate how far-reaching the Lord's School Zone is. Why, he can even use hardship as a scholarship to higher learning.

Les, his sister, and four brothers learned how to work hard. Under the severe tutelage of their father, they often did the work of adults. In sometimes treacherous weather, in extreme temperatures for unending hours, they worked in the northern woods of Michigan cutting pulp.

Today they all have sterling reputations as tireless workers and good providers. So even though their upbringing was harsh, they took away an important life lesson; work hard and reap the bounty of your labor.

Les learned other lessons as well. His heart has remained tender toward kids caught in difficult or hurtful situations who act out

their anger in rebellion. Once, while directing a Christian conference center, he became involved with an alternative high school
program that was meeting on the grounds.

Les noticed that many of the students didn't take the time to
eat, which made it difficult for them to stay focused throughout
the day. So he decided he wanted to provide breakfast for them.
The school officials were grateful for Les's help, but they didn't
believe the kids would make the effort to come early just to eat.
The program was a surprising success; even the teachers showed
up. Les prepared the food himself. The kids' favorite was the
McLes's—egg, bacon, and cheese on a bun. For his involvement,
Les was presented with the "Most Outstanding Citizen and Edu-
cator of the Year" award by the city's school system.

I about popped my petunias with pride. To think he took
painful feelings from his past and turned them into supportive
efforts to benefit others—now that's what I call making the grade.

I finally made the grade myself, graduating from high school
(two years after my son Marty graduated) just before my fortieth
birthday. What a relief to have the testing over with so I could get
on with the joy of learning. And that is what learning has become
for me—a joy. I now believe that as long as there is breath in the
body there are lessons to be learned, truths to be integrated, trust
to be deepened, and faith to be expanded.

My Mamaw (grandmother) made the grade in a different
way. She was ninety-seven years old when she died. Her graduate
school was a nursing home. Her final lessons were on relinquishment, grace, and closure. Tough curriculum. And while our resistance to these topics won't change the outcome, it will impact the
quality of our existence and the style with which we exit.

When I exit this life, I'd like to go out like Elijah in a fiery
chariot. However, I become ill on amusement park rides, so what's
the chance I could handle a flaming float harnessed to a flying stal-
lion? Truth be known, I get nauseous riding the carousel swan.

No, perhaps I'd prefer to be like Enoch who walked with God, and he was not, for God took him (see Genesis 5:24). Imagine, here one moment and gone the next. Sort of a whodunit mystery. Except I'm hoping for a big funeral with party hats, horns, and confetti. If nobody can find me, they might call off the celebration.

Well, there's always Lazarus. What a coming out party that would be. Except I'm not much on grave clothes. I wonder if they even come in petite sizes.

Well, I guess I'll leave the graduation exercise up to the Teacher and keep directing my attention to the lessons.

Seventeen

Slow Down

Luci Swindoll

Every change of scene is a delight.
—SENECA

Our days are numbered. We know that, although we usually avoid thinking about it. Life, with its demands, has a way of sapping our energy so little inclination is left to anticipate the future or the quiet life. We just want to make it through the day.

From the moment we're born, our experiences shape us into the persons we become. However, we seem always to be working at learning how to live but rarely living. We are each allotted a certain number of days on this earth, but we never seem to find the time to put into practice what we've spent a lifetime learning. What a pity.

Why do we race so much? What drives us? Where are we going so fast? I have never been one to rush around. In fact, one reason I love being Texan by birth is that we're well known for our two speeds: slow . . . and stop. We lollygag at the supermarket, wander through the shopping mall, hang out in the neighbor's backyard, or sit on the front porch at sundown drinking coffee and eating watermelon. We have lived by an inner rule of thumb that says, "I ain't goin' nowhere because this is the place to be. If I stay here, I don't have to hurry." I'd rather be at an airport an hour before my departure time, just so I don't have to hustle my bustle. And my very favorite exercise is a brisk sit.

Some folks would call this lazy, but I call it wisdom. After all, the Bible teaches in Psalm 90 that the days of our years are seventy, or maybe eighty at best, and full of labor and sorrow. Then we are gone; we "fly away." In verse 12, the psalmist adds, "So teach us to number our days that we may get a heart of wisdom" (RSV). Listen to how Eugene Peterson expresses these verses in his book, *The Message*: "We live for seventy years or so (with luck we might make it to eighty), and what do we have to show for it? Trouble. Toil and trouble and a marker in the graveyard. . . . Oh! Teach us to live well! Teach us to live wisely and well!"

Amen, brother. I believe the Bible is telling us, in great part, to "slow down." This road sign needs neither interpretation nor translation. It means exactly what it says: Reduce your speed. When we ignore or disobey this sign, we may well be in harm's way up the road . . . or put someone else in danger. This sign is a warning to take heed, watch out, exercise more caution than usual. The same tenet applies when we number our days on the journey of life. We adjust our speed in an effort to slow down and live wisely.

Several years ago I read a story that often comes to mind when I think about the wisdom of taking life slowly.

It seems that some African missionaries had hired a number of native workers to carry their supplies from one village to another. The missionaries, possessed of the American "push-rush-hurry" mentality, verbally prodded their native employees every day to go a little faster and a little farther than they had the day before. Finally, after three days of being pushed and hurried, the native workers sat down and refused to move.

"What in the world is the problem?" the American missionaries wanted to know. "We have been making excellent time. There's no need to stop here."

"It is not wise to go so rapidly," the spokesman for the native workers explained. "We have moved too fast yesterday. Now today we must stop and wait here for our souls to catch up with our bodies."[1]

Don't you love that? ". . . Wait here for our souls to catch up with our bodies." What a powerful philosophy. So many believe the slowing down time of life is up ahead, during retirement years, but what about those persons who never make it to retirement? When will their souls ever catch up? Although retirement provides an opportunity to reevaluate one's life, the time for slowing down is today.

Lily Tomlin says, "For fast-acting relief, try slowing down." Simply put, take a few minutes daily to ponder what is worthwhile about living. Stop whirling about like a pinwheel long enough to come to a rest and consider your next action. Just what is it you want to do? What do you need to do for the sake of your soul?

Pausing for a moment here and there takes conscious effort, especially at first, but it will eventually become a habit, and the habit will turn into a way of life. In fact, it will most probably become a foundation stone in one's value system, because we simply cannot live fully or wisely without slowing down, without putting on the brakes, without awareness of each moment.

Four or five years ago my brother Chuck bought a bike . . . but not just any bike. It was a Harley-Davidson. And not just any Harley, but a low rider that could race across the world at breakneck speeds. He loves the thing. He and his wife, Cynthia, ride for

---

[1]Paul Borthwick, *101 Ways to Simplify Your Life* (Wheaton, Ill.: Victor Books, 1992), 68–69.

hours with their Harley-loving friends. It is not uncommon for these two to show up at speaking engagements, family gatherings, or church meetings on the Harley. The bike is always polished to the point my brother can see his face reflected in the chrome. He maintains a consistent, loving relationship with that machine.

In keeping with family tradition, I decided about a month ago that I, too, needed a bike. So I found an appropriate shop, went in, told them what I wanted, and came away with the bicycle of my dreams: a Hampton Classic . . . no speeds, no gears, no chrome. It is beautiful—white with white sidewalls, front and rear lights, oogah horn, a little basket, and a battery-operated fan. And what a delight to ride. At least once a day I pedal through my quiet neighborhood—either in the early morning or later in the day as the sun is setting. I watch the changing clouds in the sky, the hot-air balloons floating overhead, the mountains silhouetted across the horizon, the ducks playing on the ponds, and the rosebuds coming to full bloom. I wave to or chat with friends in their golf carts, going off to the green. On a hot evening I might even encounter a full-blowing sprinkler and ride through it to cool off. I sing, I pray, I reflect back on the days when I was fourteen and had my first bike.

The other day, I even took my cellular phone along on my ride and called my friend on her cellular phone as she traveled across Arkansas. "Hello! Bicycle to car, bicycle to car." Gosh, that was fun!

It would never occur to me to buy a Harley-Davidson. I can't imagine wanting to go anywhere that fast. When I see Chuck riding it, I always think, "Babe, slow down." My motto is: Keep it simple, slow, easy, and ramblin' . . . whatever permits me to either "slow or stop" without having to think too fast. My friend Mary gave me a little sign that captures my preference in a nutshell: "Anything for a quiet life."

Philosophically speaking, the road sign Slow Down implies something that at times is even more important than "reduce speed." That is to "take time"—to enjoy your family and friends, to see beauty, to discover yourself, to have fun, to commune with God. When we slow down, we discover more opportunities for these activities because we've cleared a space in our lives for them.

When I was in college my art instructor, Marion Hebert, told us that the study of art would teach us to look at life in a different way. By virtue of wanting to see all that was in front of us, we would be forced to slow down, take time, be deliberate—in short, to *think*. She would say, "A piece of art is what *you* make it. Whether or not it is good art by the world's standards doesn't really matter. What matters is that you put yourself into it, that you paint what *you* see or draw what *you* feel, not the duplication of what has already been done. Take your time. Listen to what is inside you and spring off that. Have fun with it. Making something from scratch is fun. It is a pleasure, so find pleasure in it."

Ah, pleasure. What a wonderful thought. Don't you love to do or be in something pleasurable? It makes the soul content.

About three years ago, the art major in me decided to make something with my hands, some little art object. I've found this pastime pleasurable since childhood. I love making things, and I love owning things that are handmade. I went into my little studio (which contains a drafting table and chair and all the tools needed to accomplish great artistic feats) and picked up one of my favorite books, *Spooner's Moving Animals or The Zoo of Tranquillity* by Paul Spooner. It shows the reader how to make the most interesting, automated animals. The anteater's tongue flies out of its mouth, the goat eats grass and paper hot water bottles, the lion cries "Roar," the woodpecker scoots down a tree trunk, etc.

I couldn't wait to start creating one of these creatures. Three days later, with Spooner's paper cut-out design, thread, glue, toothpicks, and a lot of loving labor, *voila!* There was my little goat, standing on a cardboard rock. Turn the lever, and her mouth moves from left to right, munching on the blades of green grass and the red water bottle. My little masterpiece!

Now, I know, *nobody cares!* This is an inane, eccentric way to spend one's time. But of course, that's the whole point. Nobody has to care but me. That *I* care, find fun in what I make, and enjoy it to this day is what matters. The look on my friends' faces when I ask them, "Wanna see my automated goat?" is worth the whole project.

You see, it's not what we *do* with our private time that matters so much, it's that we see the importance of making room for the time in the first place. I may not understand *why* you have chosen to spend your leisure as you have, but I can respect that you find leisure important.

Isak Dinesen, in her book, *Out of Africa*, mentions that moving slowly is of utmost importance to the African. He doesn't like to hurry. The author describes it this way:

> Natives dislike speed, as we dislike noise, it is to them, at the best, hard to bear. They are also on friendly terms with time, and the plan of beguiling or killing it does not come into their heads. In fact, the more time you can give them, the happier they are, and if you commission a Kikuyu to hold your horse while you make a visit, you can see by his face that he hopes you will be a long, long time about it. He does not try to pass the time then, but sits down and lives.[2]

That beautiful passage reflects something that we in America have lost in our penchant for racing around. Our desire to accomplish, succeed, make a name for ourselves or a million dollars before we're fifty causes us to forfeit the joy of real living. Would that we, on our respective journeys, could somehow bottle

---

[2]Isak Dineson, *Out of Africa* (New York: Random House, Inc., 1937, 1952), 244.

up that plan of not "beguiling or killing" time and learn to appreciate every minute as it rolls around, simply because it is a gift from the Almighty Creator.

Another by-product of slowing down and taking time is that we get to know ourselves better. We discover who we are, accept who we are, and find the freedom to be who we are. Decreasing the amount of time we spend on things in our exterior world gives us the opportunity to increase the amount of time we spend cultivating our interior world. Therein lies an enormous value in slowing down. But this work is very hard.

When I was growing up, I had no idea who I was. Yes, I was a Swindoll, and a daughter, and a sister to two wonderful brothers, but I didn't know the me inside my own skin. Every now and then someone asks me if I would like to be in my twenties again. I can readily answer, "Absolutely not!" I have no desire to repeat those years of inner debates, confusion, insecurity, fear, and all that accompanies one's individuation. They were the hardest years of my life. I wasn't even at the threshold of learning what life was all about. I was somewhere out on the periphery, struggling with my identity and my actions and reactions.

My mother used to say, "It takes a lifetime to learn how to live … and then it's too late." There's a lot of truth in that—unless at some point we "apply our hearts unto wisdom," and genuinely ask the Lord what he would have us do to become acquainted with who we really are.

The year my mother died, 1971, I did that very thing. I told the Lord I was tired of being some anonymous person to myself, not knowing what I really believed or valued, and that I would appreciate it very much if he would help uncover and unravel the real *me* inside. I consciously began this quest twenty-five years ago, and the Lord has been answering that prayer all this time. It is not always easy to understand his revelations, and the pursuit of knowing myself has often left me lonely and discouraged. Nevertheless, on my journey I have come to realize his grace is sufficient for anything I have ever faced or ever will face in this life. As the author of the hymn says, "Through many dangers, toils and snares I have already come. 'Tis grace has brought me safe thus far, and grace will lead me home."

What has truly enriched this search for myself are those times I've set aside for solitude. Solitude is the ability to be alone without being lonely. It is finding my personal space and living there, whether or not I'm flat broke, whether or not the phone rings, whether or not I like myself. Solitude forces me to take a strong look at my life and determine whether I want to remain in a particular stage of development forever or ask the Lord to help me move forward.

I read a tidbit about solitude the other day that said living alone is just like being married—except the relationship you have is with yourself. Like marriage, living alone has its ups and downs. Sometimes you hate yourself, and sometimes you love yourself. There are days you find yourself fascinating and days you find yourself an intolerable pain ... And, here is where my little analogy falls apart. Because one thing you can't do alone, as in marriage, is to stalk into the other room and slam the door in your face.[3]

Oh, I don't know about that. A few days ago I made a pot of coffee, then went on a walk as it was brewing. What I didn't know was that I had not "seated" the pot correctly in the coffeemaker when I left. When I returned, I found dark liquid oozing over the top of the pot and down the counter.

I gave myself a little lecture: "Keep your cool, Luci. This is not the end of the world. Just mop it up and go on with your day." I reached for a towel, but my hand accidentally struck a glass vase sitting on the counter, which sailed to the floor and broke into ... yes, I would say this is accurate ... a million pieces. By this time,

[3]Jeffrey Kottler, *Private Moments, Secret Selves, Enriching Our Time Alone* (Los Angeles, Calif.: Jeremy Tarcher, Inc. by St. Martin's Press, 1990), 34.

I was considering running away from home and letting the children clean up the mess ... only to remember I was unmarried and living alone. So, I thought, *I can be flexible. I'll just drink a glass of milk instead of coffee.*

I reached into the refrigerator for the milk carton, but a glass container of honey sat in front of it. As I pulled out the milk, the honey tumbled out, too, hitting the floor and shattering on impact.

Neither time nor space permit the capturing of my total range of actions here, but they begin with something like, "As I was setting fire to the house ..." No, that wasn't my response. Actually, I laughed and laughed and laughed. I was almost out of control when I spotted the honey heading across the kitchen floor and under the stove. Jarred to my senses, I spent the next forty-five minutes swabbing and mopping. And I can tell you, had there been a door to my kitchen, I would have stalked out of the room and slammed that door in my face. That would have felt wonderful!

So living alone has its pros and cons. By the way, I am not advocating one pursue solitude to the exclusion of intimacy. Each is important to achieve balance, and without one, the other is not as meaningful. But solitude forces us to be more productive, more independent, more responsible, more reflective than we would be otherwise. It causes us to face ourselves and accept ourselves, spilled honey and all.

One final note about slowing down. This may come as a surprise to you, but I like growing older. In fact, I like being the age I am, sixty-four. I really do. I no longer have to prove anything or feel I have to accomplish every objective I've ever had. I'm not driven to correct every wrong I see. Someone has said, "In youth we learn; in age we understand," and while I may not understand everything about life, I do know a great deal more than I did in my twenties or thirties or even forties. I laugh easily and don't take myself too seriously. I don't sweat the little things. When I look in the mirror, I see more than aging skin or an expanded waistline.

Inside that reflection I see a child who wants to play, create, and discover new projects or joyful events. And the mind under that bleached blond hair is just bursting to read a new book, explore fascinating conversations with friends, and tackle a different way to plant or grow flowers in a desert garden.

It's now, in my retirement years, that I am facing brand-new vistas. At the age of sixty-one I took out a thirty-year loan to buy my first home. At sixty-two, I bought a fully loaded, dynamite computer with so many bells and whistles it'll take me years to comprehend its workings. At sixty-three, I took my first African photo safari. And now, at sixty-four, I'm about to enter into a business venture designing stickers with Andrea Grossman. In many ways, the fun is just beginning.

It's never too late to dream or to start something new. You may have reared your family or completed a career—or never had a career. You may not be as advanced in age as I am, but even in the "prime" of life you may feel that you've lived past your dreams. You may be discouraged because they didn't come true. And as much as you'd like to, you can't turn around and repeat your journey, no matter how many regrets you may have. God has put in each of us a sort of biorhythmical clock, a spiritual mechanism, if you will, that ticks away every day, reminding us that *this is it*. This is your life. And so, while you may not have slowed down, you've *shut* down. You've stopped.

Let me say to you, there's no need for that. Some of your happiest (dare I say even most productive) years are ahead of you on this journey of joy. Julia Child said, "A passionate interest in what you do is the secret of enjoying life, perhaps the secret of long life, whether it is helping old people or children or making cheese or growing earthworms."[4]

---

[4]Charlotte Painter and Pamela Valois, *Gifts of Age* (San Francisco, Calif.: Chronicle Books, 1985), 79.

In Ecclesiastes 3, the wisest man who ever lived, Solomon, expounds on the times and seasons of our lives and how they all fit together. Life is not some vague process of subtle, illogical patterns placed willy-nilly in our path for us to puzzle over. It's a composite of definitives: joys and sorrows, gains and losses, giving and keeping, laughing and grieving, loving and losing … on and on until the last numbered day arrives. But the part I really love about this passage is Solomon's admonition to slow down, savor life, take time.

"So I conclude that, first, there is nothing better for a man than to be happy and to enjoy himself as long as he can; and second, that he should eat and drink and enjoy the fruits of his labors, for these are gifts from God" (Eccl. 3:12–13 TLB).

As you have read through the pages of this book and considered the road signs along the way, you've seen that your life is no different than Barbara's, Marilyn's, Patsy's, or mine. We've all experienced detours, roadblocks, dead ends, even no-way-outs.

Like you, we are simply trying to learn to yield, wait, anticipate, be careful, slow down, speed up, move over, take an alternate route or, in some cases, just pull off the road and rest awhile. We don't claim to have all the answers to the questions life presents on this journey. It's a sojourn of faith. A pilgrimage. But what a comfort to know that in every circumstance Jesus cares. He cares about each of us. He goes before us and with us and behind us, providing a soft shoulder to lean on, loving arms to buckle ourselves into, and ample light to illumine the dark roads ahead.

And, best of all, because Jesus cares, he gives us joy for the journey, rest along the way, laughter in the midst of sorrow, and hope for the future. That thought puts a smile on my face. How about yours?

WOMEN OF FAITH [SM]

The *Joyful Journey* is based on the popular
Women of Faith conferences.

Women of Faith is partnering with Zondervan
Publishing House, Integrity Music, *Today's Christian Woman*
magazine, and Campus Crusade to offer conferences,
publications, worship music, and inspirational gifts that
support and encourage today's Christian women.

Since their beginning in January of 1996, the Women of
Faith conferences have enjoyed an enthusiastic welcome
by women across the country. Women of Faith conference
plans presently extend through the year 2000.
Call 1-888-49-FAITH for the many conference
locations and dates available.

See following pages for additional information
about Women of Faith products.

www.women-of-faith.com

More for Your Joyful Journey...

The Joyful Journey
Audio Pages
ISBN: 0-310-21454-8

With trademark warmth and humor, the authors share selections from their book about the obstacles, bumps, and detours we sometimes face along the journey of life and about how friendship, laughter, and celebration can help steer our hearts closer to God.

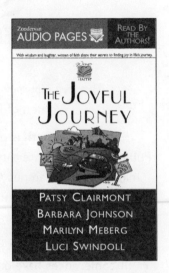

The Joyful Journey
Perpetual Calendar Daybreak
ISBN: 0-310-97282-5

Three hundred sixty-six encouraging and inspiring excerpts from the book by Patsy Clairmont, Barbara Johnson, Marilyn Meberg, and Luci Swindoll celebrate life and bring joy and laughter every day of the year!

Devotions for Women of Faith

Joy Breaks
Patsy Clairmont, Barbara Johnson, Marilyn Meberg, and Luci Swindoll
ISBN: 0-310-21345-2

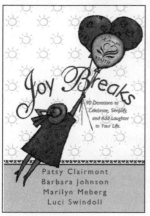

Ninety upbeat devotionals that motivate and support women who want to renew and deepen their spiritual commitment. These devotions illustrate practical ways to deepen joy amidst all the complexities, contradictions, and challenges of being a woman today. Women of all ages will be reminded that any time, any day, they can lighten up, get perspective, laugh, and cast all their cares on the One who cares for them.

Joy Breaks Daybreak™
ISBN: 0-310-97287-6

Bring joy to your life every day with 128 light-hearted, inspiring, and joyful devotional excerpts from the book *Joy Breaks*.

Available at Christian bookstores everywhere!

ZondervanPublishingHouse
Grand Rapids, Michigan

hhtp://www.zondervan.com or AOL keyword ZON

Gifts Designed for Women of Faith

*O Lord, You will fill me with joy
in your presence.*—Acts 2:28

Women of Faith Journal
ISBN: 0-310-97634-0
A perfect place to express your thoughts, reflect on
devotions, and record favorite prayers and memories.

Enamel Lapel Pin (1998 Theme)
ISBN: 0-310-97638-3

Women of Faith Mug
ISBN: 0-310-97635-9

Promises of Joy for a Woman of Faith Gift Book
ISBN: 0-310-97389-9

Words of Wisdom for a Woman of Faith Gift Book
ISBN: 0-310-97390-2

Prayers for a Woman of Faith Gift Book
ISBN: 0-310-97336-8

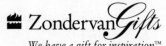

We have a gift for inspiration™

Grand Rapids, Michigan

A Division of Harper Collins Publishers
hhtp://www.zondervan.com or AOL keyword ZON

New from Women of Faith!

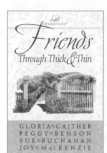

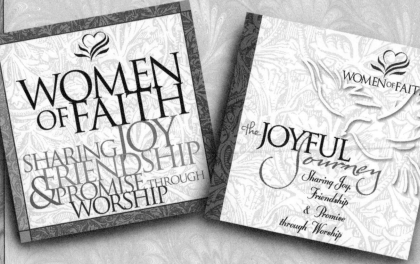

We want to hear from you. Please send your comments about this book to us in care of the address below. Thank you.

ZondervanPublishingHouse
Grand Rapids, Michigan 49530
http://www.zondervan.com